BE KEEPERS
CULTIVATING A GODLY LIFE

LISA IVEY WALLER

21ST CENTURY CHRISTIAN

Be Keepers
ISBN: 978-0-89098-952-4

©2025 by 21st Century Christian, Inc
Nashville, TN 37215
All rights reserved.

No part of this publication may be reproduced, stored in a retrieval system, or transmitted in any form or by any means—electronic, mechanical, photocopy, recording, digital, or otherwise—without the written permission of the publisher.

Unless otherwise indicated, all Scripture quotations are taken from the New King James Version® (NKJV®). Copyright © 1982 by Thomas Nelson, Inc. Used by permission. All rights reserved.

Scripture quotations marked (NASB®) are taken from the New American Standard Bible® (NASB®), Copyright © 1960, 1962, 1963, 1968, 1971, 1972, 1973, 1975, 1977, 1995, 2020 by The Lockman Foundation. Used by permission. All rights reserved. lockman.org"

Scripture quotations marked (KJV) are taken from the King James Version. Public domain.

Cover design by Jared Kendall

Be Keepers is dedicated to the memory of my mother, grandmothers, and mother-in-law who loved and served the Lord all the days of their lives and to my daughter, daughters-in-law, and granddaughters in the expectant hope that they will ever be diligent keepers of God's Word.

With cherished memories of Barbara Ivey, Prussia Campbell, Mauda Ivey, Elsie Dalla-Santa, and Sylvia Waller.

In loving encouragement of Sara, Brandy, Karen, Katy, and Eloise Hutson; Ellen, Morgan, Lois, and Vivian Waller.

TABLE OF CONTENTS

FOREWORD 7

UNIT ONE: BE KEEPERS OF YOURSELVES 9
- **LESSON 1** Be Keepers of His Commandments 11
  - BEE-ATTITUDE: LIVE FOR OTHERS 12
- **LESSON 2** Be Good 23
  - BEE-ATTITUDE: DO GOOD TO BE GOOD 24
- **LESSON 3** Be Pure 35
  - BEE-ATTITUDE: STRIVE FOR PURITY 35
- **LESSON 4** Be Obedient 49
  - BEE ATTITUDE: OBEY WILLINGLY 49

UNIT TWO: BE KEEPERS AT HOME 65
- **LESSON 5** Be Godly Wives 69
  - BEE-ATTITUDE: WORK TOGETHER 69
- **LESSON 6** Be Loving Mothers 87
  - BEE-ATTITUDE: LOVE YOUR CHILDREN 87
- **LESSON 7** Be Hospitable Homemakers 99
  - BEE-ATTITUDE: EXTEND HOSPITALITY 99

UNIT THREE: BE KEEPERS OF HIS CHURCH 109
- **LESSON 8** Be Followers 115
  - BEE-ATTITUDE: FOLLOW WILLINGLY 115
- **LESSON 9** Be Encouragers 133
  - BEE-ATTITUDE: ENCOURAGING 133
- **LESSON 10** Be Workers 147
  - BEE-ATTITUDE: PURPOSEFULLY DILIGENT 147

UNIT FOUR: **BE KEEPERS OF THE FAITH** 157

LESSON 11   Be Counted Worthy... 161
   BEE-ATTITUDE: WORTHINESS.. 162

LESSON 12   Be Deemed Courageous 175
   BEE-ATTITUDE: COURAGE.. 176

LESSON 13   Be Found Watchful 191
   BEE-ATTITUDE: WATCHFULNESS 191

EPILOGUE: BE LOVERS OF GOD'S WORD 215

APPENDIX: HOW-TO LESSON FOR ANNOTATING TEXT 217
REFERENCES... 221
ENDNOTES 223

FOREWORD

The title of *Be Keepers* is borrowed from the commendation in Titus 2:5 for women to *be keepers at home* (KJV) or *be homemakers* (NKJV). The title also appeals to Scriptures that teach us to *be* virtuous women who *keep* His commandments. Its goal is that women of all ages and stages of life in Christ will learn to better apply biblical wisdom to live more joyful, abundant, and purposeful lives.

Each lesson compares virtuous living to the wisdom our Creator instilled in the honeybee. The Proverbs encourage us to consider the ways of God's tiny creatures. Chapter 30 describes ants that gather food for winter, conies that live in the safety of rocky crags, and spiders that skillfully weave their webs even in kings' palaces.[1] These allegories teach us to prepare, use discretion, take initiative, and trust God's wisdom. Similarly, each lesson in *Be Keepers* links facts about God's amazing honeybee to His perfect plan for our lives.

The heart of each study is an examination of God's Word: His commands for godly living with examples from Scripture where His will was obeyed, neglected, or defied. Discussion questions, Psalms, songs, and topics for prayer are suggested to edify those who study together and glorify our Heavenly Father. Please pray for *wisdom* as you study: not mere knowledge held in the head but understanding that proceeds from the heart to put your faith into action.

Wishing you grace and peace in our Lord Jesus Christ!

Lisa

UNIT ONE

BE KEEPERS OF YOURSELVES

*"But you, beloved,
building yourselves up on your most holy faith,
praying in the Holy Spirit,
keep yourselves in the love of God,
looking for the mercy of our Lord Jesus Christ
unto eternal life."*

Jude 1:20–21

UNIT ONE INTRODUCTION

BE KEEPERS OF YOURSELVES

Lessons 1-4 teach what it means to *keep yourself in the love of God*, beginning with three inseparable tenets of Christianity:

- *Love God,*
- *Love God's children,*
- *Keep God's commandments.*

In 1 John 4:10-11 Christian love is defined, "*In this is love, not that we loved God, but that He loved us and sent His Son to be the propitiation for our sins. Beloved, if God so loved us, we also ought to love one another.*" In the first lesson, Christian love is tied to obedience, "*By this we know that we love the children of God, when we love God and keep His commandments. For this is the love of God, that we keep His commandments. And His commandments are not burdensome.*"[2]

We cannot separate loving God from loving one another, nor love from obedience.[3] Living as God commands gives our lives purpose. Do you want to live a purposeful life? Keep His commandments. God commands us to ensure that our family and neighbors are not doing without food, clothing, care, or the knowledge of His will.[4] Jesus says His commandments are not burdensome. When we call ourselves by Jesus' name and do His work, we glorify God and truly live the good life!

LESSON ONE

BE KEEPERS OF HIS COMMANDMENTS

*"By this we know that we love the children of God,
when we love God and keep His commandments.
For this is the love of God, that we keep His commandments.
And His commandments are not burdensome."*

1 John 5:2-3

BE KEEPERS

Christians are to love God, love one another, and keep God's commandments. We cannot do one without the others. Examine these critical attributes of our faith from 1 John 5:2-3.

"By this we know that we love the children of God," pinpoints loving others as the essence of Christianity. Jesus said, "By this all will know that you are My disciples, if you have love for one another."[5]

"When we love God and keep His commandments," identifies loving God and keeping God's commandments as Christians' essential responsibility. When asked, "Teacher, which is the great commandment in the law?" Jesus said, *"'You shall love the LORD your God with all your heart, with all your soul, and with all your mind.'*[6] *This is the first and great commandment. And the second is like it: 'You shall love your neighbor as yourself.'*[7] *On these two commandments hang all the Law and the Prophets."*[8]

All of God's commands address our actions toward Him and/or other people. We spend our time and talents in many temporal pursuits, but God's Word directs us toward the spiritual aspects of living: our relationship with God who is spirit and our relationships with other people who are eternal souls. As we keep His commandments, our possessions, time, and talents are used for spiritual purposes to His glory. His commandments "are not burdensome" because they are perfect directions from our Creator for living the purposeful lives that He created us to live!

BEE-ATTITUDE: LIVE FOR OTHERS

Successful beekeepers, apiarists, allow honeybees to do what they were created to do with minimal interference. These amazing insects can operate a healthy, honey- producing hive because each bee does the work God designed a honeybee to do. Worker bees feed the larvae and queen bee, secrete wax to build the honeycomb, and stock its cells with food for winter. Queen bees do not direct the workers, but mate once with male drone bees and spend the rest of their lives laying the eggs needed to keep the colony viable.

Each bee's life contributes to the success of the hive. A queen bee may lay 2,500 eggs a day and live for more than three years. Successful drones die right after the mating flight.

Worker bees live brief but busy lives of five to eight weeks. Yet, a healthy honeybee colony may continue indefinitely because their collective efforts ensure that new bees mature and assume the work as older bees decease.

Like honeybees, God wants each of us to live as He created us to live. When we keep the faith and mature in our spiritual lives, we have a positive influence on those around us. **No one lives to himself or dies to himself**.[9] That is true both physically and spiritually. Do you wish to love God and love others? God says we love Him and our neighbors when we keep His commandments. Therefore, we must do the work we were created to do and teach others to do the same. When individual Christians live as God purposed, the church thrives. It is the everlasting kingdom of God![10]

GOD'S WISDOM

The Bible gives factual accounts of the lives of men and women. It speaks with equal candor of human failures and courageous demonstrations of faith, showing how objectively God can see and judge mankind.[11] The history of Israel's transition from the period of judges to having human kings is told in 1 Samuel. Chapters 1-4 record the negative influence of Eli's godless sons and the positive impact of the God-fearing family of Elkanah on the people of Israel.

Eli was Israel's High Priest. He had two adult sons, Hophni and Phinehas. They served with him in the tabernacle but were vile men. When people came to make offerings, they robbed God by taking more than their share of the sacrifices. Eli's sons also fornicated with women who helped care for the tabernacle. **No one lives to himself**. Hophni and Phineas' sins caused the people of Israel to abhor offering to the Lord. The people told Eli of his sons' evil works, but Eli failed to restrain them.[12] The Israelites began to transgress God's laws out of fear and resentment of Eli's sons.

Angered, God foretold and later fulfilled His judgment against Eli's household, removing them permanently from the priesthood. In one day, God allowed the Philistines to kill both Hophni and Phinehas who had brought the ark of the covenant into a battle. The Philistines also took the ark of God and killed 30,000 Israelites. A messenger told Eli that his sons were killed, and the ark had been taken. When Eli heard that the ark of God had been captured, he fell backward off his seat and died of a broken neck.[13] When Phineas' wife was told, she went into labor and died just after giving birth.[14] **No one dies to himself**. Eli and his sons did not obey God's commands. Their sins destroyed their own family and tragically affected the nation of Israel.

In contrast, 1 Samuel also tells of Elkanah's family. His wife, Hannah, endured taunting from his second wife over her childlessness. Yet, Elkanah loved Hannah without concern that she was barren. Hannah took her heartache to God in prayer at the temple to ask for a son. She vowed to entrust him back to God and fulfilled her promise by taking young Samuel to live in the tabernacle and serve under Eli.[15] Samuel grew in favor with God and the people. God blessed him, and the people soon recognized Samuel as God's prophet and judge. Scripture says that Samuel judged Israel faithfully all his life. He anointed Saul and David as kings by divine command, always faithfully delivering God's message. **No one lives a godly life to himself, either.** How differently the obedient lives of Elkanah, Hannah, and Samuel affected Israel!

KEEP YOURSELF IN THE LOVE OF GOD

When a woman keeps herself in the love of God, she allows His plan to direct her steps. She keeps herself from sin, studies God's Word, prays continuously, and trusts His will for her life. Deuteronomy 4:9 emphasizes that it is a deliberate, lifelong endeavor to keep yourself in the faith, *"Only take heed to yourself, and diligently keep yourself, lest you forget the things your eyes have seen, and lest they depart from your heart all the days of your life. And teach them to your children and your grandchildren."*

Hannah did not set out to influence the fate of Israel or the billions of people who have since heard, read, and been encouraged by her example of faith. She sought to keep herself in God's love. She turned to God in fervent prayer to relieve her anguish and took comfort in Eli's promise that God would answer. She did what she vowed to do, though it must have been terribly difficult to see Samuel only once each year. She knew God's command, *"Hear, O Israel: The LORD our God, the LORD is one! You shall love the LORD your God with all your heart, with all your soul, and with all your strength."*[16] Hannah demonstrated her love of God by keeping her unusual promise, but also by obeying His commandments day to day.

A wonderful passage, 2 Peter 1:2-11, clarifies what it means to keep ourselves in God's love, to make our calling and election sure. Read and make notes in the table below. (See Appendix 1, How to Annotate the Text.)

2 PETER 1:2-11

"Grace and peace be multiplied to you in the knowledge of God and of Jesus our Lord, as His divine power has given to us all things that pertain to life and godliness, through the knowledge of Him who called us by glory and virtue, by which have been given to us exceedingly great and precious promises, that through these you may be partakers of the divine nature, having escaped the corruption that is in the world through lust.

But also for this very reason, giving all diligence, add to your faith virtue, to virtue knowledge, to knowledge self-control, to self-control perseverance, to perseverance godliness, to godliness brotherly kindness, and to brotherly kindness love. For if these things are yours and abound, you will be neither barren nor unfruitful in the knowledge of our Lord Jesus Christ.

For he who lacks these things is shortsighted, even to blindness, and has forgotten that he was cleansed from his old sins. Therefore, brethren, be even more diligent to make your call and election sure, for if you do these things you will never stumble; for so an entrance will be supplied to you abundantly into the everlasting kingdom of our Lord and Savior Jesus Christ."[17]

LOVING GOD'S CHILDREN IS KEEPING HIS COMMANDMENTS

Christian women love God's people by keeping His commandments, *"Owe no one anything except to love one another, for he who loves another has fulfilled the law. For the commandments, 'You shall not commit adultery,' 'You shall not murder,' 'You shall not steal,' 'You shall not bear false witness,' 'You shall not covet,' and if there is any other commandment, are all summed up in this saying, namely, 'You shall love your neighbor as yourself.' Love does no harm to a neighbor; therefore love is the fulfillment of the law."* [18]

If we love someone, we value them above temporal things, forgoing liberties to protect their souls. We do not covet what they have, gossip about them, nor use them to fulfill our lusts. We see that they have the care, food, clothing, and knowledge of God they need. We seek their good before our own. We edify our sisters and brothers in their spiritual walk. In Romans 14:1, 7-8 we are told, *"Receive one who is weak in the faith, but not to disputes over doubtful things… <u>For none of us lives to himself, and no one dies to</u> himself. For if we live, we live to the Lord; and if we die, we die to the Lord. Therefore, whether we live or die, we are the Lord's."*

The Book of Romans was first written as a letter to Jewish Christians who lived in Rome. They were struggling with eating meat sold in the marketplace that had been offered to idols when many of their Gentile brethren had been converted from idolatry. Paul asks, *"But why do you judge your brother? Or why do you show contempt for your brother? For we shall all stand before the judgment seat of Christ. For it is written: 'As I live, says the Lord, Every knee shall bow to Me, And every tongue shall confess to God.' So then each of us shall give account of himself to God. Therefore let us not judge one another anymore, but rather resolve this, not to put a stumbling block or a cause to fall in our brother's way."*[19]

Just before His crucifixion, Jesus gave the apostles a direct command to love and serve one another. He had just given them the unforgettable example of service as He washed the disciples' feet, modeling the humility with which we are to serve one another. Jesus spoke with clarity and passion to prepare them for His crucifixion and the events that would follow. Chapters 13-25 of the Gospel of John record Jesus repeatedly commanding His disciples to love one another and keep His commandments. Jesus Christ offered His love of God, love of all people, and obedience unto death as examples for us to follow. Read and make notes next to the Scripture that follows.

JOHN 15:9-17

"As the Father loved Me, I also have loved you; abide in My love. If you keep My commandments, you will abide in My love, just as I have kept My Father's commandments and abide in His love. These things I have spoken to you, that My joy may remain in you, and that your joy may be full.

This is My commandment, that you love one another as I have loved you. Greater love has no one than this, than to lay down one's life for his friends. You are My friends if you do whatever I command you. No longer do I call you servants, for a servant does not know what his master is doing; but I have called you friends, for all things that I heard from My Father I have made known to you.

You did not choose Me, but I chose you and appointed you that you should go and bear fruit, and that your fruit should remain, that whatever you ask the Father in My name He may give you. These things I command you, that you love one another." [20]

When we obey Jesus' command to love others, we must not allow temporal things to interfere with our mission of saving souls nor forget the price our Lord paid. When customs of the Greeks and Jewish Christians clashed, food was repeatedly an issue. Paul helped them set priorities, *"Yet if your brother is grieved because of your food, you are no longer walking in love. Do not destroy with your food the one for whom Christ died."* [21] Likewise, we are to put others before self as did our Lord; *"Let nothing be done through selfish ambition or conceit, but in lowliness of mind let each esteem others better than himself. Let each of you look out not only for his own interests, but also for the interests of others."* [22]

God's people promote the kingdom when they do in their daily living what God teaches. Elkanah did not set out to bless the nation of Israel when he gave Hannah a double portion to assure her that he did not resent her childlessness. He showed a husband's love when he begged her to lift her spirits and eat, trying to be better to Hannah than 10 sons. Elkanah's faith in God and love of his wife even allowed him to support her vow to give Samuel to serve God.[23] God used Elkanah's obedience to bless Israel.

When we keep ourselves in God's love, we do not flaunt our blessings or scorn the less fortunate as did Elkanah's second wife, Peninnah. We do not covet what does not belong to us, fulfill our lusts by taking advantage of vulnerable people, neglect disciplining our children, or make ourselves 'fat' by defrauding God as did Hophni, Phinehas, and Eli.

When we love one another, we are obeying the second greatest commandment, *"You shall love your neighbor as yourself."*[24] Our obedience can bring glory to God and blessings to our families and the church. We can even uplift our communities and nations.

LOVING OUR ENEMIES IS KEEPING HIS COMMANDMENTS

Christianity differs from human philosophies because our love for others includes those who wrong us. Consider four reasons for this. First, God is our Father who sends rain on the just and the unjust. We should be like God, our Father.[25] Second, we have all sinned and been redeemed by the immeasurable grace of our Lord. How can we condemn others when we have been forgiven of such debt?[26] Third, all of mankind is in a battle against the devil and sin. The people who seem to be our enemies have been ensnared in his traps. Still, they are God's creation, our neighbors, our sisters, and brothers. They share our temptations and brief lives. Like us, they have no hope but Jesus Christ, so we are to pray for them.[27] Finally, if we wish to be forgiven, we must forgive others.[28] Vengeance belongs to the Lord.[29]

When considering how to treat those who oppose us, it is equally important to know what a godly woman does *not* do. Romans 12:14 says, *"Bless those who persecute you; bless, and do not curse."* Hannah did not take vengeance against Peninnah. She did not blame her husband for her rival's antagonism. When Eli approached Hannah, supposing her to be intoxicated because she moved her lips without making a sound, Hannah explained that she was praying in anguish. Hannah did not become angry about Eli's accusation or decide to never go to worship again. We are told, *"Let all bitterness, wrath, anger, clamor, and evil speaking be put away from you, with all malice. And be kind to one another, tenderhearted, forgiving one another, just as God in Christ forgave you."*[30]

LOVING GOD IS KEEPING HIS COMMANDMENTS

This study will examine Titus 2:4-5 (KJV) several times. First, focus on the reason it gives for women to live godly lives. *"That they (older Christian women) may teach the young women to be sober, to love their husbands, to love their children, To be discreet, chaste, keepers at home, good, obedient to their own husbands,* **that the word of God be not blasphemed***."* Eli's sinful sons blasphemed God's laws and caused the Israelites to abhor giving to God because they profaned His tabernacle. Christians must set a godly example, lest we risk others' souls. It is treasonous to be called by Jesus' name but defy His Word. If we do, we bring reproach upon the church, which is not a building or human institution. The church is the body of Christ. The church is the kingdom of God. It includes our brothers, sisters, Jesus Christ, God the Father, and the Holy Spirit![31]

Hannah's exemplary obedience in difficult circumstances remains valuable to you and me. When Hannah brought Samuel to the tabernacle to live, she prayed a prayer that was guided by the Holy Spirit and included a Messianic prophecy. We can read her inspired song in 1 Samuel 2:1-10 and Mary's allusions to it in Luke 1:48-55. While keeping herself in the love of God, Hannah became part of God's preparation to send Christ through the lineage of David whom her son, Samuel, anointed as king of Israel.

When we love God and obey His commandments, we can advance His kingdom, the church of Christ. We must keep ourselves unspotted from the world. We must worship and adhere to God's Word. We must teach the truth to others and care for our neighbors. When we are doers of the Word, we preserve a faithful congregation of the Lord's church for the next generation. Jesus says that His Word and His church are everlasting.[32] Like honeybee hives, church congregations thrive when they are composed of faithful, diligent workers who lovingly prepare younger Christians to keep His commandments and do the work of the church.

SEVEN-POINT DISCUSSION GUIDE

1. Give an example of how keeping God's commandments shows your love of God. Is this always true?

2. Give an example of how keeping God's commandments shows your love for others. Is it possible to truly keep God's commands without learning to love others?

3. Refute False Teaching: Some people teach that God determined our eternal fate before the world began. However, Romans 14:13 says that we can put a cause to fall in our brother's way. Romans 14:15 cautions that we can destroy one for whom Christ died. How does this contradict that false doctrine?

4. How might someone in the church cause a newer Christian to fall away? How might pride, fear, ambition, or worldly lusts motivate one to discourage another Christian? What is the consequence for causing a little one, a novice in the faith, to fall?[33]

5. How do we prepare younger Christians to do the work of the church? How might we improve in this work in our congregation and families?

6. What actions might you take this week to keep yourself in the love of God?

7. We are to be keepers of God's new covenant in Jesus Christ. What blessings does come to those who keep His covenant, according to Psalm 103:15-18?

SONG AND PSALM

"LOVE ONE ANOTHER"

PSALM 103:15-18 NKJV
"As for man, his days are like grass;

As a flower of the field, so he flourishes. For the wind passes over it, and it is gone, And its place remembers it no more.

But the mercy of the Lord is from everlasting to everlasting On those who fear Him,

And His righteousness to children's children, To such as keep His covenant,

And to those who remember His commandments to do them."

SUGGESTED TOPIC FOR PRAYER
Pray for God's help in understanding His Word and will for our lives. Ask for the courage to be keepers of His commandments and to imitate His grace, mercy, and peace.

BE KEEPERS

LESSON TWO

BE GOOD

"He has shown you, O man, what is good;
*And what does the L*ORD *require of you But to do justly,*
To love mercy, And to walk humbly with your God?"

Micah 6:8

Mothers call after their children, "Be good!" in hope that they will do the right thing when they are away. Our Heavenly Father wants us to be good. Even before Adam and Eve were able to discern good from evil, the devil set to work to blur the distinction.[34] What is good? Human philosophies claim it varies with the situation. This is untrue. Good is defined by the very nature of God who does not change.[35] Therefore, what is good also remains unchanged by the devil's lies, circumstances, or the values and laws of diverse cultures.

God's Word says young women should be taught to be good.[36] The world constantly perverts the truth. It is necessary for us to look only to God for our standards. The prophet Micah wrote that the good required of us is to do justly, love mercy, and walk humbly with our God.[37] This lesson will examine these aspects of Christian living.

BEE-ATTITUDE: DO GOOD TO BE GOOD[a]

Honey is fine food for bees, bears, or people! It tastes good and is good for you. It contains all the substances needed to sustain life. It is a source of pinocembrin, an antioxidant with anti-inflammatory properties. Honey is a potent source of energy. Just one ounce could power a bee's flight all the way around the world!

Honey is antimicrobial because of its low moisture, high concentration of sugars, and a small amount of hydrogen peroxide that is created in a bee's honey production process. Thus, sealed honey is an effective wound treatment and never spoils.

Honeycombs found in Egyptian tombs had remained unspoiled in sealed containers for over 2,000 years.[a] No wonder God encouraged the Israelites with the promise of a land that flowed with milk and honey!

Christian women are to do good to be godly. We are to conduct ourselves in ways that bless those around us and glorify God.[38] Christian women imitate our sinless Lord Jesus Christ.[39] Our righteousness is not of ourselves but comes from the grace of God, who alone is good.[40] We have the gift of eternal life because God has sealed us by His Holy Spirit.[41] Just as God led the Israelites to the Promised Land that flowed with milk and honey, Christ has gone to prepare a home for us where all will be joy, peace, and goodness.[42]

WHAT IS *GOOD*?

Jesus taught that only God is good. *"Now a certain ruler asked Him, saying, "Good Teacher, what shall I do to inherit eternal life?" So Jesus said to him, "Why do you call Me good? No one is good but One, that is, God."*[43] Of course, Jesus Christ is the Good Teacher, but He seems to have said this to challenge whether this man was confessing belief in Him as the Son of God.

No one is good but God (the Father, Son, and Holy Spirit), so how can we be commanded to be good? We can be sanctified as blameless because of Christ's atonement for our sins: *"Now may the God of peace Himself sanctify you completely; and may your whole spirit, soul, and body be preserved blameless at the coming of our Lord Jesus Christ."*[44] Our sins

---

[a] To view Egyptian hieroglyphics depicting beekeeping, please visit https://www.loe.org/shows/segments.html?programID=15-P13-00046&segmentID=7."

are washed away when we put on Christ in baptism, and we do good when we imitate Christ.[45]

When our precious Lord Jesus was on His last journey to Jerusalem, knowing His crucifixion was imminent, He passed through Samaria. Early in His ministry, Jesus had told the woman at Jacob's well that He was the Christ and many Samaritans had believed on Him.

However, Luke tells us that on this visit the people rejected Jesus because He was determined to go on to Jerusalem.[46] Like the Jews who called for Jesus to be put to death a few days later, these Samaritans held to the traditions of their fathers rather than accepting Jesus as Christ.

The apostles were indignant and asked Jesus if they should call down fire from heaven to consume the Samaritans. They were referring to Elijah's actions 900 years before when Ahaziah, the king of Samaria, sent messengers to inquire of the idol Baal instead of God.[47] Jesus reacted differently than the apostles expected, *"But He turned and rebuked them, and said, "You do not know what manner of spirit you are of. For the Son of Man did not come to destroy men's lives but to save them."*[48] Likewise, we are to love and do good to others.

> *"Now may the God of peace who brought up our Lord Jesus from the dead, that great Shepherd of the sheep, through the blood of the everlasting covenant, make you complete in every good work to do His will, working in you what is well pleasing in His sight, through Jesus Christ, to whom be glory forever and ever. Amen."*[49]

We can know what manner of Spirit we serve! God has shown us what is good and requires that we do justly, love mercy, and walk humbly with Him.[50] We can look to Scripture for examples in the lives of others who have served our Holy God.

JUSTICE, MERCY, AND HUMILITY

When God had Samuel anoint Saul as commander and king over Israel, some people opposed his leadership.[51] Soon after he was anointed as king, the territory of Jabesh-Gilead came under siege. Saul brought three companies of fighters together and won a decisive battle against the Ammonites. Afterward, some people called for the execution of those who had opposed

Saul and refused to fight, but by mercy Saul said, *"Not a man shall be put to death this day, for today the LORD has accomplished salvation in Israel."*[52]

Saul's godly example of mercy was returned later when he had exacted an oath from the people to eat nothing on a day when they were going into battle against the Philistines. Scripture says Saul was seeking vengeance against the Philistines, so he said he would execute anyone who broke the vow. Perhaps vengeful emotions clouded Saul's judgment. His eldest son, Jonathan, was commanding a portion of the army but was unaware of his father's edict.

> "But Jonathan had not heard his father charge the people with the oath; therefore he stretched out the end of the rod that was in his hand and dipped it in a honeycomb and put his hand to his mouth; and his countenance brightened. Then one of the people said, "Your father strictly charged the people with an oath, saying, 'Cursed is the man who eats food this day.'" And the people were faint.
>
> But Jonathan said, "My father has troubled the land. Look now, how my countenance has brightened because I tasted a little of this honey. How much better if the people had eaten freely today of the spoil of their enemies which they found! For now would there not have been a much greater slaughter among the Philistines?"[53]

When the day ended, Saul could get no answer from God. He asked God to cast a perfect lot to show who had offended, and the lot fell on Jonathan.

> "Then Saul said to Jonathan, "Tell me what you have done." And Jonathan told him, and said, "I only tasted a little honey with the end of the rod that was in my hand. So now I must die!"
>
> And Saul answered, "God do so and more also; for you shall surely die, Jonathan." But the people said to Saul, "Shall Jonathan die, who has accomplished this great deliverance in Israel? Certainly not! As the LORD lives, not one hair of his head shall fall to the ground, for he has worked with God this day." So the people rescued Jonathan, and he did not die."[54]

The people demanded mercy for Jonathan because he had worked with God to deliver Israel from their enemies. Perhaps they realized that God had shown mercy for Israel in the conflict. Perhaps they were encouraged by the mercy King Saul had previously extended to those who opposed him as king. Saul had shown mercy out of respect for the victory God had given him in his first battle. Christians are merciful because of the immeasurable mercy we have received from Christ. Just as tasting the honey brightened Jonathan's countenance, the sweet example of mercy demonstrated by God's people enlightens others. When we see someone exemplify the goodness of God's nature, we understand what is required of us to be like Him.

DO JUSTLY

The Bible offers many wonderful examples of justice and mercy for us to follow, but none are greater than that of Jesus Christ. Though He is God, He humbled Himself to live and die for men and women because we are all condemned by our sins. The Scriptures in the table below admonish us to be good by doing justly. As you read, make notes about what each Scripture reveals:

DO JUSTLY — RELATED SCRIPTURES

"My brethren, do not hold the faith of our Lord Jesus Christ, the Lord of glory, with partiality. For if there should come into your assembly a man with gold rings, in fine apparel, and there should also come in a poor man in filthy clothes, and you pay attention to the one wearing the fine clothes and say to him, "You sit here in a good place," and say to the poor man, "You stand there," or, "Sit here at my footstool," have you not shown partiality among yourselves, and become judges with evil thoughts?" [55]	

"'Cursed is the one who perverts the justice due the stranger, the fatherless, and widow.' And all the people shall say, 'Amen!'" [56]

"To do righteousness and justice Is more acceptable to the LORD than sacrifice." [57]

"It is a joy for the just to do justice,
But destruction will come to the workers of iniquity." [58]

"Evil men do not understand justice,
But those who seek the LORD
understand all." [59]

"Thus says the LORD of hosts:
'Execute true justice,
Show mercy and compassion Everyone to his brother." [60]

"Blessed are the merciful,
For they shall obtain mercy." [61]

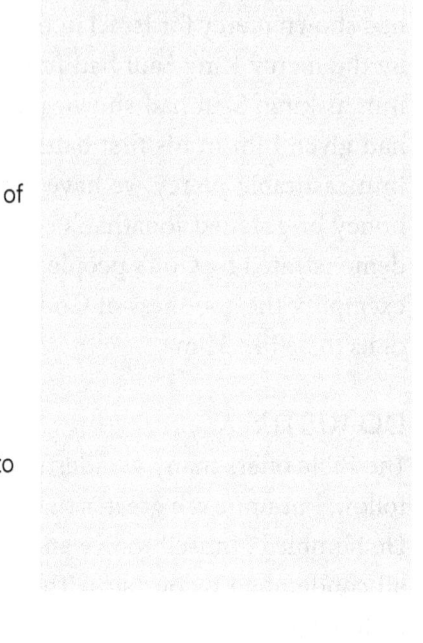

LOVE MERCY

God will judge each person's soul to determine his or her eternal destiny. Therefore, condemnation and vengeance are not our responsibilities. God is merciful, full of grace and patience. Jesus Christ, the Son of God in the flesh, died to make our salvation possible. We are to be the light of the world, reflecting His nature. We are to seek to deliver others from sin. We are to love mercy and pray for God's mercy on ourselves and others. We are to be like God, Christ, and the Holy Spirit. In the table below are scriptures about what we do to love mercy and why it is important. As you read, make notes about what each of the scriptures reveals.

SHOW MERCY — RELATED SCRIPTURES

"Blessed are the merciful,
For they shall obtain mercy." [61]

"For judgment is without mercy to the one who has shown no mercy. Mercy triumphs over judgment." [62]

"And when he heard that it was Jesus of Nazareth, he began to cry out and say, "Jesus, Son of David, have mercy on me!" [63]

"So which of these three do you think was neighbor to him who fell among the thieves?" And he said, "He who showed mercy on him." Then Jesus said to him, "Go and do likewise." [64]

"But God, who is rich in mercy, because of His great love with which He loved us, even when we were dead in trespasses, made us alive together with Christ (by grace you have been saved), and raised us up together, and made us sit together in the heavenly places in Christ Jesus, that in the ages to come He might show the exceeding riches of His grace in His kindness toward us in Christ Jesus." [65]

"Brethren, do not be children in understanding; however, in malice be babes, but in understanding be mature." [66]

"But the wisdom that is from above is first pure, then peaceable, gentle, willing to yield, full of mercy and good fruits, without partiality and without hypocrisy." [67]

"But love your enemies, do good, and lend, hoping for nothing in return; and your reward will be great, and you will be sons of the Most High. For He is kind to the unthankful and evil. Therefore be merciful, just as your Father also is merciful." [68]

WALK HUMBLY WITH YOUR GOD

We learn to walk humbly with God when we realize that our will is a poor substitute for God's will. Though we imagine our plans to be best for us, God's love is perfect, and His knowledge is complete. His plans are always superior.[70] Mary, the mother of Christ incarnate, is an amazing example of humility before God. She was engaged to Joseph and had plans for her life, as would any young woman. Yet, Mary overcame fear and was not misled by pride. Read Luke 1:26-38:

> "Now in the sixth month the angel Gabriel was sent by God to a city of Galilee named Nazareth, to a virgin betrothed to a man whose name was Joseph, of the house of David. The virgin's name was Mary. And having come in, the angel said to her, "Rejoice, highly favored one, the Lord is with you; blessed are you among women!"
>
> But when she saw him, she was troubled at his saying, and considered what manner of greeting this was.
>
> Then the angel said to her, "Do not be afraid, Mary, for you have found favor with God. And behold, you will conceive in your womb and bring forth a Son, and shall call His name JESUS. He will be great, and will be called the Son of the Highest; and the Lord God will give Him the throne of His father David. And He will reign over the house of Jacob forever, and of His kingdom there will be no end."
>
> Then Mary said to the angel, "How can this be, since I do not know a man?"
>
> And the angel answered and said to her, "The Holy Spirit will come upon you, and the power of the Highest will overshadow you; therefore, also, that Holy One who is to be born will be called the Son of God. Now indeed, Elizabeth your relative has also conceived a son in her old age; and this is now the sixth month for her who was called barren.
>
> For with God nothing will be impossible."
>
> Then Mary said, "Behold the maidservant of the Lord! Let it be to me according to your word." And the angel departed from her."

Mary had the humility to be the *"maidservant of the Lord"* and the faith to accept Gabriel's message that she was to be highly favored and blessed among women. Mary's trust in God displaced any fear of what it would mean to be found with child before her marriage. Joseph, her fiancé, considered divorce before an angel appeared to him in a dream. Public humiliation and stoning were the punishment for fornicators under the Law of Moses.[71] Still, Mary was willing to walk humbly with her God.

Everything Mary had imagined about her life was changed, but pride did not deter her either. This young woman's faith did not falter when she had to deliver her baby, Jesus, in a stable. It did not fail when she and Joseph fled to Egypt to save Jesus from King Herod or when they moved to Nazareth for safety during Archelaus's rule. Her humility was not lost to pride when Jesus' divinity became apparent to the world. Even at Jesus' crucifixion, when most of the apostles fled, Mary stood nearby.

We are all sinners but have pardon in the grace of Jesus Christ who died on that cross for our sins![72] When we are baptized into Christ, we put on Christ, and His blood continually washes us of our sins. We receive the gift of the Holy Spirit, eternal life, and are preserved blameless if we walk in the light.[73] Micah 6:8 says we are to walk humbly with our God. *Walk* here means living our daily lives in accordance with His perfect will. Read Romans 12:14-21 and note what each of these verses reveals about walking humbly with our God.

WALK HUMBLY — ROMANS 12:14-21

Bless those who persecute you; bless and do not curse.

Rejoice with those who rejoice, and weep with those who weep. Be of the same mind toward one another.

Do not set your mind on high things, but associate with the humble.

Do not be wise in your own opinion. Repay no one evil for evil.

Have regard for good things in the sight of all men. If it is possible, as much as depends on you,

live peaceably with all men. Beloved, do not avenge yourselves,

but rather give place to wrath; for it is written, "Vengeance is Mine, I will repay," says the Lord. Therefore "If your enemy is hungry, feed him;

If he is thirsty, give him a drink;

For in so doing you will heap coals of fire on his head."

Do not be overcome by evil, but overcome evil with good.[74]

SEVEN-POINT DISCUSSION GUIDE

1. God took the throne away from King Saul's family because he repeatedly sinned against God. What excuses did Saul give Samuel in chapters 13 and 15?

2. False Teaching: Some people teach situational ethics, that right and wrong are not fixed and sin is acceptable in particular circumstances. What do the messages Samuel delivered to King Saul in 1 Samuel chapter 13 and 15 suggest about this lie?

3. Have you been hurt by another person's injustice? How did that affect your feelings and actions toward others? When might a Christian woman be called upon to do justice in her daily life?

4. When have you been the recipient of mercy from another person? How did that affect your thinking? How did it affect your feelings and actions toward others?

5. Walking humbly with God means to submit to His will in our daily lives. Whether it is fear or pride that motivates a person's disobedience, it

reveals the absence of trust in God. When might we be guilty of offering partial obedience to God?

6. When Micah said that God has shown man what is good, he addressed our attitudes toward others (justice and mercy) and our attitude toward God (humility).

   Social psychology recognizes that attitudes are:
   1) affected by our knowledge, beliefs, and emotions,
   2) typically learned from others,
   3) changed only through persuasion and self-reflection, and
   4) the basis for our actions.

   What does this suggest about the importance of the Scriptures and the church of Christ in our lives?

7. Psalm 34:11-14 says that if we desire a good, long life, we must do good! What does it say we do not do?

CALL TO ACTION
What good can you do this week as an individual or as a group of Christians to glorify God and show love for Him and others?

SONG AND PSALMS

JUST A CLOSER WALK WITH THEE

PSALM 34:11-14
"Come, you children, listen to me;
I will teach you the fear of the Lord.
Who is the man who desires life,
And loves many days, that he may see good?
Keep your tongue from evil,
And your lips from speaking deceit.
Depart from evil and do good;
Seek peace and pursue it.

PSALM 111:10
"The fear of the Lord is the beginning of wisdom;
A good understanding have all those who do His commandments.
His praise endures forever."

SUGGESTED TOPIC FOR PRAYER
Pray for God's guidance to be like Him, for He alone is good! Thank God that He is just, merciful, and willing to direct our steps. Pray for the grace to be just and merciful to others and to walk humbly before our God.

LESSON 3

BE PURE

*"Since you have purified your souls in obeying the truth
through the Spirit in sincere love of the brethren,
love one another fervently with a pure heart,
having been born again, not of corruptible seed but incorruptible,
through the word of God which lives and abides forever."*

1 Peter 1:22-23

Christian women must learn to be **pure**.[75] Purity is defined by what is excluded. Sin is excluded from the life of a Christian. Human doctrines have no place in worship of the Lord. Sexual immorality is not to be committed with a body wherein the Holy Spirit dwells. Envy and covetousness do not reside in a righteous heart. The abominations of idolatry are not practiced by those who are purified by Christ. Jesus taught the importance of the purity commanded by God, *"Blessed are the pure in heart, For they shall see God."*[76]

BEE-ATTITUDE: STRIVE FOR PURITY

Commercial beekeepers lease-out and ship whole hives of bees to farms and orchards just in time for a crop's pollination. Bees sip nectar from blooms on the plants and pack pollen into pouches formed by hairs on their back legs for a source of protein.

Some pollen clings to hair on top of their bodies and is brushed off on the flowers' stigma to fertilize seeds and help fruits and vegetables form. This arrangement assures an abundant crop for the farmer and honey for the beekeeper. Some pollen makes its way into the honey as the bees deposit it in the honeycomb. Although pure honey will contain pollen, it should have no additives or contaminants.

Adulterated honey is a great concern to the industry. To increase profits, some unscrupulous producers extend honey with sugar water or corn syrup. Impure honey spoils easily and may not be fit to eat. By law in the U.S., a product that is impure cannot be labeled as honey. Shopping for *Pure Honey* on a label is important, but the law is not easily enforced so the consumer must choose honey from a reliable source to ensure its purity.

Christians must remain pure from the world to be worthy of the name of Christ. When the Book of Life is opened, God's law will be fully enforced.[77] We are to abstain from fornication and idolatry, practice pure religion, and worship in Spirit and in truth to be pleasing to God.

There is no place in the life of a Christian man or woman for sexual immorality or covetousness, which is idolatry. Practicing religion that is adulterated with the doctrines of men is not true Christianity. The only source for the pure will of God is His own Word. We will each answer for ourselves before God. Therefore, we must diligently defend against the pollutants of this world!

KEEP YOUR HEART PURE

When Jesus taught, *"Blessed are the pure in heart, For they shall see God,"*[78] He spoke to the desire to see God that has always filled the hearts of the faithful. Jesus Christ's preaching had a revolutionary focus on the heart as He called mankind to repentance. Yet study of the Old Testament reveals that God has always insisted that our hearts be pure. Christ emphasized that all of God's commandments tell us how to love God and love others. Jesus' doctrine in the New Testament presses us to examine the motives that drive our actions because our words and actions manifest the thoughts of our hearts.

God's people desire to see Him. The prophet Isaiah wrote, *"Your eyes will see the King in His beauty; They will see the land that is very far off."*[79] John opens his Gospel affirming that the Word of God came in the flesh and dwelt among us! He witnesses, *"That which was from the beginning, which we have heard, which we have seen with our eyes, which we have looked upon, and our hands have handled, concerning the Word of life..."*[80] John says, *"No one has seen God at any time. The only begotten Son, who is in the bosom of the Father, He has declared Him."*[81] John did not describe Jesus' appearance but characterizes the Son of God as full of grace and truth![82] The hope of seeing Him as He is motivates us to live pure lives.

> *"Behold what manner of love the Father has bestowed on us, that we should be called children of God! Therefore the world does not know us, because it did not know Him. Beloved, now we are children of God; and it has not yet been revealed what we shall be, but we know that when He is revealed, we shall be like Him, for we shall see Him as He is. And everyone who has this hope in Him purifies himself, just as He is pure."*[83]

Standing before God's throne and beholding His holiness will be overwhelming for every man and woman. We will each be aware of our own sinful past. The Bible tells of the reactions of men who realized they were in God's presence. One was Peter who had been fishing all night on Galilee with his partners but were coming in without success on the morning that Jesus called him to discipleship. When Jesus told Peter to cast the nets again, they drew out a miraculous catch of fish. Luke 5:8 says, *"When Simon Peter saw it, he fell down at Jesus' knees, saying, "Depart from me, for I am a sinful man, O Lord!"*

Both the prophet Isaiah and the apostle John were given visions in which they stood before God. The prophet declared, *"Woe is me, for I am undone! Because I am a man of unclean lips, And I dwell in the midst of a people of unclean lips; For my eyes have seen the King, The LORD of hosts,"*[84] and an angel used a coal of fire to cleanse his lips. About 750 years later, John saw and recorded God's Revelation. The last book of the New Testament tells us that when the apostle John saw the glorified Christ, he fell at His feet as dead but was raised up by Christ's hand.[85]

Christians are purified by the sacrifice of Jesus Christ who knew no sin when we repent of our sin, confess our belief in Jesus as the Son of God, become washed in the blood of Christ in baptism, and are raised to walk in newness of life.[86] We are commanded to be pure as He is pure.[87] If we sin, we must confess our sin, and the blood of Christ will continue to cleanse us of sin.[88] By living in Christ-like purity, we prepare to meet our God.[89] Hebrews 10 tells how Christ's sacrifice makes it possible for us to come into God's presence, to enter the Holiest.

HEBREWS 10:12-23

"But this Man, after He had offered one sacrifice for sins forever, sat down at the right hand of God, from that time waiting till His enemies are made His footstool. For by one offering He has perfected forever those who are being sanctified. But the Holy Spirit also witnesses to us; for after He had said before, "This is the covenant that I will make with them after those days, says the LORD: I will put My laws into their hearts, and in their minds I will write them," then He adds, "Their sins and their lawless deeds I will remember no more." Now where there is remission of these, there is no longer an offering for sin.

Therefore, brethren, having boldness to enter the Holiest by the blood of Jesus, by a new and living way which He consecrated for us, through the veil, that is, His flesh, and *having* a High Priest over the house of God, let us draw near with a true heart in full assurance of faith, having our hearts sprinkled from an evil conscience and our bodies washed with pure water. Let us hold fast the confession of *our* hope without wavering, for He who promised *is* faithful."[90]

PURE FROM WORLDLINESS

In a lesson about purity, you may anticipate a discussion of Christian women dressing modestly, preserving their chastity, and keeping a civil tongue. All Christians need purity, our sons as well as our daughters; the old as well as the young. A woman's purity of life is a manifestation of having her heart right with God. Peter taught that our hearts are purified by faith,[91] and that results in loving one another with a pure heart.[92] Again, we see that loving God, obeying God, and loving one another are inseparable.

Our dress is to be neither seductive nor pretentious. We must not try to draw attention to ourselves with immodest or costly garments nor assume roles in the home or church that God assigned to men.[93] Christians must not encourage others to lust or covet by our dress or actions. Instead, Christian women are to concentrate on doing good works that glorify God.[94] We are to be like our Lord. Jesus Christ did not come to earth in a form that attracted people to His physical appearance but lived a life of godliness so that we are drawn to Him for the truth of His message and the hope of salvation in Him.[95]

Proverbs 31:30 cautions, *"Charm is deceitful and beauty is passing, But a woman who fears the* L<small>ORD</small>, *she shall be praised."* In dressing and conducting ourselves as commanded by God through the inspired writings of the apostles, we submit to the perfect will of God. The world rejects the God-given roles for women, but we are to be the light of the world.[96] Our humility and obedience help others learn to submit to God's will.[97]

Chastity is demanded by God to keep us from sin.[98] The purity of a virgin bride for her husband and fidelity in marriage are used throughout Scripture to compel Israel and the church to be spiritually faithful unto God. The church is the bride of Christ. Infidelity will cost us our salvation.[99] Under the old law, fornication and adultery were punishable by stoning. However, Christ did not come to judge the world but to teach us to repent, so He did not condemn the adulteress who was brought to Him but told her to go and sin no more.[100] Our Lord used her blatant sin to make her accusers see the sin in themselves, for He came to preach repentance and holiness.[101]

We will be judged by what proceeds out of our mouths. Our speech is to be seasoned with salt to preserve a positive influence on non-Christians.[102] Paul told the Colossians, *"But now you yourselves are to put off all these: anger, wrath, malice, blasphemy, filthy language out of your mouth. Do not lie to one another, since you have put off the old man with his deeds and have put on the new man who is renewed in knowledge according to the image of Him who created him."*[103] God's Word is truth. God does not lie and hates a lying tongue.[104] The devil is the father of lies and was a liar from the beginning.[105] Gossip and scorn ought not cross our lips.[106] Our voices should be used to praise God and edify one another, not to curse and condemn others.[107]

Good things will come from our lips when our hearts and minds are focused on things that are true, honest, just, pure, lovely, of good report, virtuous, and praiseworthy.[108] *"For He said, "Surely they are My people, Children who will not lie." So He became their Savior."*[109]

PURE FROM FORNICATION

We are to *"Flee also youthful lusts; but pursue righteousness, faith, love, peace with those who call on the Lord out of a pure heart."*[110] In keeping ourselves pure from fornication and adultery, we preserve an example of the relationship God desires with His church. That light on a lampstand is desperately needed! Although intimacy has its rightful place inside marriage, this section will focus on the impurities that we must aggressively guard against.

Sexual sin is a great part of the reason our society has fallen. As a child, I remember my vigilant mother clicking her tongue when the TV showed a man and woman kiss. Oh, how things have worsened! Turn off the television every time you are shown fornication or adultery. The screen won't be on long. Mission accomplished. Be careful what you put into your mind with books, shows, music, and idle chatter.

Ladies ... lust is not love. Infatuation is not love. Butterflies in your stomach are a reaction of the autonomic nervous system to a stressful situation. When you get anxious, your body releases adrenaline and reroutes blood from your stomach to your limbs for fight or flight. Butterflies are constricting stomach muscles, not a litmus test for locating your true love. Sex is not love. Getting nervous around someone of the same gender is not an indication that you were "born gay" either. Disney lies to you. News media lie to you. The internet lies to you. Advertisements, Hollywood, the music industry, and your streaming videos lie to you.

Separate lust from your thinking about relationships. Married men and women must also realize the danger of filling our homes with the devil's images and lies. The internet and streaming services can bring gross and perverted images and more into your home without ringing the doorbell. Sexual relations outside the bond of marriage are sins against God. Even consensual interactions are wrong and misuse others for satisfaction of physical desires. A Christian must rule over sin, control her physical body *"in sanctification and honor, not in passion of lust."*[111] Sexual activities can dominate and destroy your reputation, health, spiritual life, family, careers, health, and cost your soul. If you are caught up in such activities, repent, turn from them, seek help if you need it from a Christian counselor. Distance yourself from temptations. Fill your life and time with good things.

Consider the following passages from God's Word.

PASSAGES ABOUT FORNICATION AND ADULTERY

"Pursue peace with all people, and holiness, without which no one will see the Lord: looking carefully lest anyone fall short of the grace of God; lest any root of bitterness springing up cause trouble, and by this many become defiled; lest there be any fornicator or profane person like Esau, who for one morsel of food sold his birthright."[112]

"Finally then, brethren, we urge and exhort in the Lord Jesus that you should abound more and more, just as you received from us how you ought to walk and to please God; for you know what commandments we gave you through the Lord Jesus.

For this is the will of God, your sanctification: that you should abstain from sexual immorality; that each of you should know how to possess his own vessel in sanctification and honor, not in passion of lust, like the Gentiles who do not know God; that no one should take advantage of and defraud his brother in this matter, because the Lord *is* the avenger of all such, as we also forewarned you and testified.

For God did not call us to uncleanness, but in holiness. Therefore he who rejects *this* does not reject man, but God, who has also given us His Holy Spirit."[113]

"Do you not know that the unrighteous will not inherit the kingdom of God? Do not be deceived. Neither fornicators, nor idolaters, nor adulterers, nor homosexuals, nor sodomites, nor thieves, nor covetous, nor drunkards, nor revilers, nor extortioners will inherit the kingdom of God.

And such were some of you. But you were washed, but you were sanctified, but you were justified in the name of the Lord Jesus and by the Spirit of our God.... Now the body *is* not for sexual immorality but for the Lord, and the Lord for the body.

And <u>God both raised up the Lord and will also raise us up by His power. Do you not know that your bodies are members of Christ? Shall I then take the members of Christ and</u> make *them* members of a harlot? Certainly not! Or do you not know that <u>he who is joined</u> to a harlot is one body *<u>with her?</u>* For *"the two,"* He says, *"<u>shall become one flesh</u>."*

But <u>he who is joined to the Lord is one spirit *with Him*. Flee sexual immorality.</u> Every sin that a man does is outside the body, but <u>he who commits sexual immorality sins against his own body.</u>

Or do you not know that your body is the temple of the Holy <u>Spirit *who is* in you, whom you have from God, and you are not your own? For you were bought at a price;</u> therefore <u>glorify God in your body and in your spirit, which are God's.</u> "[114]

PRACTICE PURE RELIGION

Purified by faith, we are to practice pure religion. *"And everyone who has this hope in Him purifies himself, just as He is pure."*[115] We are purified to do the work of God. *"Pure and undefiled religion before God and the Father is this:, visit orphans and widows in their trouble, and to keep oneself unspotted from the world."*[116] People may try to emphasize moral and doctrinal purity, but neglect works of charity and evangelism. Others may focus on benevolence and allow men's ideas to supplant God's will in the work and worship of the church. This beautiful statement of the Holy Spirit says pure religion is benevolence *and* sinless living. Hypocrites may look pure to others, but God sees the heart. He is not deceived nor swayed by man.[117] The psalmist says of God, *"With the pure You will show Yourself pure; And with the devious You will show Yourself shrewd."*[118]

God has always desired a **Holy** people to serve Him and demanded purity in His worship. When the people of Israel worshipped in the tabernacle, they were commanded to bring **pure** olive oil to burn in lamps on a **pure** gold lampstand and set 12 loaves of bread on a table of **pure** gold, sprinkled with **pure** frankincense.[119] At the Passover, they were commanded to offer a lamb **without blemish**[120] preparing Israel to understand the sacrifice of Christ Jesus, the **pure** and **sinless** Lamb of God.[121]

Worship that is designed to entertain, to cater to human pride and preference, is not pleasing to God because human additions pollute God's will.[122] God's desire for His church is given in terms of the character and actions of His people. Consider these descriptions of those who God seeks to worship Him.

A HOLY PEOPLE

Keep yourself pure, as Jesus is pure[123]
Be separate from the world, abstain from fleshly lusts[124] Draw near to God with a true heart, washed with pure water (baptized into Christ)[125]

Assemble on the first day of the week[126]
Desire the pure milk of the Word[127] Hear and do the will of God[128]

Repent and partake of the Lord's Supper worthily[129]
Worship in spirit and truth[130] Teach no other doctrine[131]

Rejoice in Christ Jesus, not in other people [132]

Love from a pure heart, a good conscience, and sincere faith [133] Share the gospel without prejudice [134]

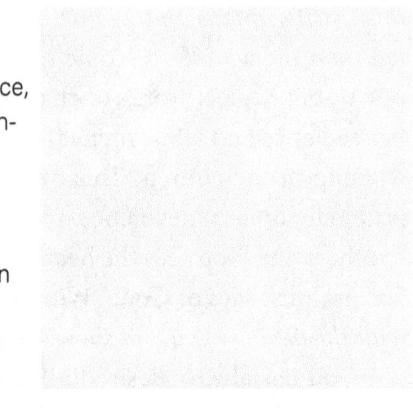

Sing to praise God and admonish one another [135]

Pray fervently with and for one another, in Jesus' name [136]

Give cheerfully, generously to the church and those in need [137]

A congregation of the Lord's church is never more than a generation away from apostasy. False doctrine and the standards of the world can destroy a congregation. Teaching the commandments of men is spiritual fornication. Young people and new converts must be taught sound doctrine and compelled to mature in the faith so they can discern God's truth from the devil's lies. The fear of God must be taught as well as the love of God and His church. Purity in our lives and worship is essential to pleasing God. Jesus Christ is the only perfect example of a sinless and pure life. Only in Him and in His doctrine can we be found pure and able to stand before God's throne!

THE COSTS OF IMPURITY

King David was faithful to God all his life. Although he sinned grievously, he was penitent and ever resolved to do God's will. God punished David when he sinned but promised to preserve his throne.[138] Prophets foretold that the Christ would come through the house of David.[139] The children of David tragically failed to keep their hearts focused upon God and the dynasty of David and Solomon over the 12 tribes of Israel was diminished, continuing only to rule the tribes of Judah and Benjamin.[140]

Their fall was because of lust for pleasure and power. King David's son, Amnon gave in to lust and raped Tamar, his half-sister. Absalom, Tamar's full brother, later murdered Amnon to avenge Tamar. Embittered, Absalom grew prideful and led an ill-fated rebellion against his father's throne.[141]

David's son, Solomon, inherited the throne and was faithful to God for much of his life. Twice, God spoke directly to Solomon insisting that he remain pure from idolatry, but in his old age, Solomon was drawn into idolatry by his hundreds of foreign wives. Because Solomon was unfaithful, God told him that the kingdom would be divided.[142]

When Rehoboam, Solomon's son, rose to the throne, he listened to his peers instead of the mature advisors of his father and levied burdensome taxes on the people. The resulting rebellion allowed Jeroboam, the son of Solomon's servant, to lead away the 10 northern tribes as God had foretold.[143] They were drawn into idolatry and suffered years in Assyrian captivity.

Judah, composed of the tribes of Judah and Benjamin, endured 70 years of Babylonian captivity.[144] Later, both Israel and Judah returned from captivity only to be subjugated by Greek and Roman rule. Judah was preserved to point the way to Jesus Christ in the lineage of David, the pure Lamb of God and anointed ruler of the Kingdom of God.[145] What a light to the world Israel might have been if the people and their leaders had remained pure hearted and obedient!

IDOLATRY

In this present era, every evil thing is put before our eyes, including idolatry, witchcraft, demon worship, and false gods. Scripture is clear that none of us can toy with evil things and have a relationship with God. It is difficult for me to imagine how a person can be seduced into worshipping an object made by men's hands. I cannot fathom why a person would think a devil could bring anything of value to their life. That is because I have been taught the truth all of my life.

My blessed childhood experience has not been the upbringing of many younger people; some immigrants; those whose college educations have robbed them of belief; or those in socialist, communist, and idolatrous nations of this world. We cannot assume that others have our prior knowledge or experiences. When we begin to teach someone the gospel, we must listen to know what that person understands and patiently teach foundational truths. We must love one another's souls enough to build a firm foundation. Jesus died for all people of all nations. Lovingly, I share the inspired Word of God, captured by David and the apostle John for you:

> *"Who may ascend into the hill of the LORD?*
> *Or who may stand in His holy place?*
> *He who has clean hands and a pure heart,*
> *Who has not lifted up his soul to an idol,*
> *Nor sworn deceitfully."*[146]

> *"Little children, keep yourselves from idols. Amen."*[147]

Do you have a neighbor who needs the gospel? Read and make notes from these verses to prepare yourself to lovingly, clearly, share the Truth.

TEACHING GOD'S COMMANDS TO OTHERS, 2 TIMOTHY 2:22-26

> "Flee also youthful lusts; but pursue righteousness, faith, love, peace with those who call on the Lord out of a pure heart.
>
> But avoid foolish and ignorant disputes, knowing that they generate strife.
>
> And a servant of the Lord must not quarrel but be gentle to all, able to teach, patient, in humility correcting those who are in opposition, if God perhaps will grant them repentance, so that they may know the truth, and that they may come to their senses and escape the snare of the devil, having been taken captive by him to do his will."[148]

SEVEN-POINT DISCUSSION GUIDE

1. False Teaching: Some say that teaching abstinence from sexual relations outside the bond of marriage is an oppression of women. How is this contradicted in Scripture?

2. Answer the question posed in Proverbs 20:9: *"Who can say, 'I have made my heart clean, I am pure from my sin,'?"*

3. Society mocks men for being virgins. As a mother and/or grandmother of boys, what message must we teach them from God's Word?

4. James 3:17 says, *"But the wisdom that is from above is first pure, then peaceable, gentle, willing to yield, full of mercy and good fruits, without partiality and without hypocrisy."* As we seek to grow in wisdom and righteousness, why is **purity** foundational to such things as **peace, kindness, humility, mercy, charity, impartiality, and sincerity**?

5. Proverbs 20:11 says, *"Even a child is known by his deeds, Whether what he does is pure and right."* How can a child learn and be held responsible for discerning what is pure and right? What things must a parent control to ensure that children are not being deceived about right and wrong?

6. Many imagine that God will not condemn a good person. If that were true, why would it have been necessary for Christ to have died? Proverbs 30:12 says, *"There is a generation that is pure in its own eyes, Yet is not washed from its filthiness."* How did this apply to the Scribes and Pharisees? How does it apply to people today?

7. First Peter 1:22-23 says, *"Since you have purified your souls in obeying the truth through the Spirit in sincere love of the brethren, love one another fervently with a pure heart, having been born again, not of corruptible seed but incorruptible, through the word of God which lives and abides forever."*

If you have been baptized into Christ, take a few moments to write down things you hope to do toward living a life that is pure. If you have not been baptized into Christ, identify the barrier that you need to overcome to obey Him.

SONG AND PSALM

PURER IN HEART

PSALM 12:6-7
"The words of the Lord are pure words,
Like silver tried in a furnace of earth, Purified seven times.
You shall keep them, O Lord,
You shall preserve them from this generation forever."[149]

PSALM 24:3-6
"Who may ascend into the hill of the Lord?
Or who may stand in His holy place?
He who has clean hands and a pure heart,
Who has not lifted up his soul to an idol, Nor sworn deceitfully.
He shall receive blessing from the Lord,
And righteousness from the God of his salvation.
This is Jacob, the generation of those who seek Him,
Who seek Your face."[150]

SUGGESTED TOPIC FOR PRAYER
Praise God for His Holiness. Thank God for Jesus' example of a holy life for us to imitate. Ask God to help us purify our hearts, giving us understanding of and what we need to become more Christ-like.

LESSON 4

BE OBEDIENT

*"How sweet are Your words to my taste,
Sweeter than honey to my mouth!*

*Through Your precepts I get understanding;
Therefore I hate every false way.*

*Your word is a lamp to my feet
And a light to my path.*

*I have sworn and confirmed
That I will keep Your righteous judgments."*

Psalm 119:103-106

In Psalm 119, the writer celebrated God's commandments as a welcome light to his path, sweeter than honey, and so compelling in righteousness that he eagerly swore obedience! When we study this masterpiece of praise, we receive instruction in righteousness and learn to treasure the opportunity for obedience!

BEE-ATTITUDE: OBEY WILLINGLY

When a worker bee locates a good source of pollen and nectar, she returns to the hive and dances, turning as she wiggles her abdomen. Her movements communicate the direction and distance to the food source. The bee will continue to dance, repeating the same moves, until others follow her directions. Bees also communicate warnings by releasing pheromones that are sensed with odor receptors on their antennae. The colony will respond quickly to these alarms. Communication is enough for bees. They follow directions to their collective benefit. Hives do not require corrections departments for disobedient bees.

Christians learn God's will through studying Scriptures, preaching, teaching, and observing the examples of more mature members of the church. Sadly, we are not as reliable as bees in our obedience of what we are told. Yet God has provided for our redemption through faith in Christ, purification in repentance and baptism, guidance through Scripture, edification in His church, strengthening in study and prayer, and discipline when we err. We have Jesus' abiding presence to help us on our journey and the blood of Christ to continually cleanse us when we confess our sin and walk in the light!

GOD'S WISDOM

Obedience is faith in action. Our faith requires us to work. Abel made an acceptable offering that pleased God, *"of the firstborn of his flock and of their fat."*[151] Throughout biblical history, sin offerings necessitated bloodshed in anticipation of the sacrifice of Jesus Christ, the only begotten Lamb of God, to redeem mankind.

Disobedience is action that originates from ungodly thoughts and does not conform to God's will. Cain's offering of grain was not pleasing to God for it did not conform to God's will, though Genesis does not record what God had commanded or why Cain's grain offering was unacceptable. When God did not accept Cain's will in place of His will, Cain was filled with anger. He was consumed with envy against Abel whose sacrifice from the firstborn of his flock had been accepted by God. God cautioned Cain, *"If you do well, will you not be accepted? And if you do not do well, sin lies at the door. And its desire is for you, but you should rule over it."*[152] Cain did not choose to rule over his anger and envy. He murdered his brother.

We must obey 'from the heart', with the sincere desire to please God.[153] Doing His will brings joy and eternal life. Unsure? Check your motives. Obedience from the heart is not feigned or done to impress men, as was the giving of Ananias and Sapphira.[154] It is not reluctant as was Jonah's preaching to Nineveh.[155] True obedience is not doing God's will only when it suits us, nor getting as close as possible to sin without crossing a line. The sincere heart will long for the joyful blessings that come from trusting God's will. It will be confident that doing so will avoid sin's painful consequences. The sincere heart will not even shrink from obedience to God when it brings persecution but will keep faith in God's promise of eternal life.

THREE BIBLICAL EXAMPLES OF OBEDIENCE

Naaman: Reluctant but Obedient

Naaman was commander of the army of the king of Syria.[156] Yet, his powerful connections could not save him from leprosy. His hope came from an unlikely place. A captive Israelite girl in his own household suggested that the prophet Elisha in Samaria could heal him. So, the king of Syria sent a letter to the king of Israel. The king felt healing the leprosy was an impossibility and a political trap, so he tore his garment. The prophet Elisha heard and told the king to send Naaman on to his house.

Naaman expected Elisha to come out to meet him and heal him in some spectacular fashion. Instead, the prophet sent word by a servant that if Naaman would wash himself in the Jordan River seven times, he would be healed. This was not what the Syrian commander thought would happen. Perhaps it lacked the pomp that came with human positions of power in which he trusted. He did not want to obey. Naaman justified his reluctance by proclaiming that there were better rivers in Damascus.

Again, help came from the humble. His servants asked gently, *"My father, if the prophet had told you to do something great, would you not have done it? How much more then, when he says to you, 'Wash, and be clean'?"*[157] At their urging, Naaman did obey God. When he came up out of the water the seventh time, not only was his leprosy gone, but his skin was like that of a child's. Obedience in humility brought the healing that Naaman needed. This is true for all people. The glory belonged to God. This is true of all glory.[158]

In the Christian age, who can help but see the parallel of Naaman's cleansing to the simple act of baptism required of us to have our deadly disease of sin washed away? Naaman's skin was not left scarred but was restored to perfection. How much greater is the miracle for all of us who have had our souls cleansed in the waters of baptism, our relationship to God restored, and the promise of eternal life bestowed through obedience to Christ's command?[159] Naaman concluded, *"Indeed, now I know that there is no God in all the earth, except in Israel"* (2 Kings 5:45). We, too, can know that salvation is only found in Jesus Christ, the Son of God.

Abraham: Tested but Obedient

Obedience is often quite difficult. Long before Naaman lived, Abraham was asked to obey in a great trial of his faith. God had never asked men for a human sacrifice. God had even promised Abraham that through his son, Isaac, He would make a great nation and bless the earth.[160] Abraham had waited until he was 100 years old for God to allow him to have a son by Sarah as God had promised. Yet, when God asked him to offer Isaac, Abraham did not argue but set out to obey the next morning.[161]

Isaac was not a small child, as some have painted him to be, but was a young adult. We know a little of what was going on in Abraham's mind as father and son journeyed to the mountain God had designated. Scriptures say he told the men that traveled with them to wait with the donkeys while he and Isaac went ahead to worship, saying, *"we will come back to you."*[162] The New Testament says that Abraham expected God to raise Isaac from the dead.[163] Isaac apparently did not resist. As you likely know, an angel of God commanded Abraham to stop only after he had bound his son on the altar and taken a knife in hand.[164]

James teaches us that we, too, must obediently act on our faith, *"But do you want to know, O foolish man, that faith without works is dead? Was not Abraham our father justified by works when he offered Isaac his son on the altar? Do you see that faith was working together with his works, and by works faith was made perfect? And the Scripture was fulfilled which says, 'Abraham believed God, and it was accounted to him for righteousness.' And he was called the friend of God. You see then that a man is justified by works, and not by faith only."*[165] God Almighty told Abraham, *"In your seed all the nations of the earth shall be blessed, because you have obeyed My voice."*[166]

Thus, Jesus Christ came as a descendant of Abraham to bring the blessing of redemption to all the nations of the earth!

Jesus: Deity but Obedient

In the fullness of time, God sent His only begotten son, Jesus, to be the sacrifice for our sins.[167] It was the fulfillment of God's incredible redemption plan that the Creator would give Himself to redeem the fallen creation! John's Gospel reveals Christ's role as the Word of God in creation, but says He took on flesh. Jesus was God in the flesh.[168] The animal sacrifices of Old Testament times did not do away with sin. Only Jesus' death on the cross could redeem mankind from the fall of Adam until the last day.[169]

As part of the godhead, Jesus has always existed, is eternal. There are many witnesses in Scripture to this truth. God proclaimed Jesus' sonship and authority at Jesus' baptism and transfiguration.[170] By inspiration of the Holy Spirit, John the Baptist proclaimed Jesus to be *"preferred before me, for He was before me"* (John 1:15) and, *"this is the Son of God"* (John 1:34). Jesus affirmed Himself as eternal, *"Most assuredly, I say to you, before Abraham was, I AM."*[171] Jesus Christ proclaimed both His divinity and His mission that was accomplished by obeying God, *"For I have come down from heaven, not to do My own will, but the will of Him who sent Me."*[172]

Hebrews 5:8 says that although Jesus was the son of God, *"yet He learned obedience by the things which He suffered."* Jesus' obedience was perfect. When He was a child, He was subject to His parents. Though sinless, he was baptized of John to fulfill all righteousness. When tempted by the devil, He held firm to the Word of God. Although He was the Son of God, when the temple taxes were due, He paid them. When rejected by religious leaders because He would not keep their traditions, He went on preaching repentance *"for the kingdom of heaven is at hand,"* the work God sent Him to accomplish.[173] Knowing He would be betrayed, falsely accused, and executed at the hands of sinful men, Jesus prayed to the Father, *"Not my will but Thine be done"* (Luke 22:42, KJV) and laid His life down to fulfill God's plan.[174] Resurrected from the grave, Jesus ascended to the throne telling His followers, *"All authority has been given to Me in heaven and on earth. Go therefore and make disciples of all the nations, baptizing them in the name of the Father and of the Son and of the Holy Spirit, teaching them to observe all things that I have commanded you; and lo, I am with you always, even to the end of the age."*[175]

Jesus said He did not speak or act of His own will, but He spoke and did the things that God the Father gave to Him![176] Jesus knew there was no reason to deviate from the will of God, for His will is inerrant and complete. If Christ Himself did not deviate from the perfect will of God, why would men or women presume to add to or take from God's plan?[177] Jesus' complete obedience provides eternal salvation to all who obey Him![178]

OUR OBEDIENCE

We also learn obedience. We learn to obey parents, obey teachers, and obey civil law. We learn to obey our employers at work and be subject to elders of the church. If we are wives, we learn to be in submission to our husbands. From the time we are small, we need to be learning to be obedient to God's Word.

In a Christian home, a child's training shows that obedience is safe because his or her mother, father, grandparents, and Jesus act out of love with the child's best interest in mind. Diligent discipline teaches responsibility.

- Diligent = parents must be consistent and work at raising a child.
- Discipline = parents teach, provide structure, model cooperation and effort, give constructive/corrective feedback, and follow-through with appropriate consequences.

Note that a parent must be diligent and self-disciplined to raise a hardworking, obedient child.

Godly examples also model the right attitude toward obedience. As a person matures, he or she recognizes that although parents' reprimands and punishments were unpleasant to experience, they were necessary to deter misbehavior and teach beneficial life lessons.[179] In the church we learn to obey God's will through preaching, teaching, Bible study, and observing the lives of faithful Christians. Then, when one becomes a mature Christian with leadership responsibilities, he or she knows to teach obedience to others while keeping themselves in submission to Christ. How important it is that Christian homes model and teach obedience!

It is not always easy to obey. Our society does not value obedience consistently. As immorality grows more prevalent in society, the virtues of godliness are increasingly belittled and defied. Obedience requires that we both trust and fear God, holding to His precepts despite social pressures. Obeying God may even require refusing to submit to human laws that go against God's law, yet it is always best for us to fear God and do His will.

Fear of men often leads to sin.[180] Emotional excuses are frequently used to justify wrongdoing, but God says, *"Listen to Me, you who know righteousness, You people in whose heart is My law: Do not fear the reproach of men, Nor be afraid of their insults."*[181]

Many people abuse power to harm others for their own gain or amusement, but the Creator of the universe humbled Himself and died to save sinners. All people in positions of responsibility face temptations to act out of ambition and selfishness, but some who claim to be Christians also neglect God's commands to leaders. When our husbands and sons are in such roles, we must support them with prayer and avoid the temptation to gossip. When women have responsibilities to teach or manage a work at church, we must do it humbly and encourage others to participate, not looking for personal recognition lest we bring reproach on the body of Christ or discourage a younger Christian. Do not lose your reward in heaven.

Godly leadership provides for the well-being of those who submit to it. It is exercised with deference to God's will and implemented with diligence. It is far more about modeling, teaching, admonishing, encouraging, structuring, redirecting, and prayer than punishment or power. Consider the leadership responsibilities of Christian men and women. Fathers are not to provoke children to wrath, but to train them to be obedient to God.[182] Mothers are to lovingly care for their children but not avoid disciplining them.[183] Indulgence is not love. Failure to correct children is to hate them.[184] Husbands are to love their wives as themselves.[185] They are told not to resent them but love and protect their wives as Christ loves the church and gave Himself for it. Employers, including slave owners, are told to do good to those they oversee, giving up threatening.[186] Elders are to know the members of their congregation, teach them, make sure they have what they need to mature in Christ, go to them and pray for them when they are sick, exhort and convict those who contradict, and watch for their souls.[187]

Whether or not those in authority are godly, we are to be obedient unless their requests are contrary to God's commands.[188] When we obey, we are to do so as unto God, as unto Christ who died for us.[189] We are to obey out of sincerity, not to impress men.[190] When we do not fulfill our responsibilities as a wife, daughter, worker, or member of a congregation, we bring reproach on the gospel.[191] The most amazing value of obedience in human relationships is that it will be rewarded as if done unto the Lord.[192]

TRIALS OF OUR OBEDIENCE

God puts us through trials to strengthen our commitment to Him.[193] Trials are challenges that we must work to meet or hold strong to endure. They invite us to be obedient despite obstacles.[194] Trials may come as mistreatment, discouragement, tragedies, or even worldly opportunities that a child of God cannot accept. Christians may be faced with trials that involve persecution, torture, or death.[195] Most of us face lesser trials of losing jobs, friends, family ties, social acceptance, or material goods when we choose to obey. Christ is always with us.[196] We do not face trials or temptations alone.[197] God often follows our times of trial with seasons of blessings as He did for Abraham. Sometimes we are called upon to be faithful unto death but are promised that all who remain faithful will see the fruits of obedience in eternity.

We must study God's Word to be ready when trials come. Scripture prepares us for tribulation. The Bible helps us prepare for the challenge by forewarning us that such trials will come, so we will continue to rely on God. The danger comes if we imagine God has abandoned us or if we yield to sin. The Old and New Testaments are filled with examples of real people who faced trials of their faith. Their lives testify to the infallibility of God's promises. They teach us to be practiced in prayer to know the Lord's abiding presence. The Scriptures reveal blessings that come from endurance as our faith is tried. They assure us that others have known similar trials.[198] They testify that the persecution our Lord experienced as the Son of Man can give us confidence that He understands our hardships and will not abandon us.[199]

Unlike trials, temptation is the pull of our lusts toward sin or the devil's efforts to get us to sin. God does not tempt us to sin.[200] Temptations certainly may come during times of trial, but God promises us a way of escape and will not let us be tempted beyond that which we are able to bear.[201] Those who yield to lusts and speak evil against those in authority will face God's judgment.[202]

SEVEN-POINT DISCUSSION GUIDE

Note: Because abortion is so heavily promoted and women have many pressures toward ungodly and unhealthy sexual relations, these questions will focus on obedience in these things. The principles discussed in this lesson can apply.

1. The word *abortion* does not occur in the Bible. How can we know God's will on the issue?

2. Deuteronomy 5:17 states the sixth commandment, "**You shall not murder.**"[203] *Shall* and *shall not* assert that something **will certainly happen** or **will certainly not happen** by the force of law. What is God communicating about the taking of another's life in this command?

3. After the flood, God gave Noah and his sons dominion over the animals and permission to eat meat without the blood in it. But God differentiated this from taking the life of a person. He warned Noah against murder and links it with the command to repopulate the earth. Notice why a man's blood is valued and the consequence for taking another person's life.

   "Whoever sheds man's blood,
   By man his blood shall be shed;
   For in the image of God
   He made man.
   And as for you, be fruitful and multiply;

*Bring forth abundantly in the earth
And multiply in it."*[204]

We are God's creation, made in His image. This is also true of the baby in the womb. The abortion industry supplies body parts from the children they kill for medical experiments and treatments. It is a multi-billion dollar a year industry that spends millions on political campaigns.

What did God give as the consequence for shedding man's blood?[205] If we are deceived by their propaganda to condone abortion, will we become partakers in the sin? Will we suffer God's wrath?[206]

4. Under the Law of Moses, God deemed taking another person's life as punishable by death as were sins of adultery, fornication, blasphemy, idolatry, and profaning the Sabbath. The Law also provided justice for the loss of an unborn baby.[207] We can see that God regards the baby as a human being from conception. Abortion is sin. Yet, Jesus Christ offers forgiveness of sin. His sacrifice can wash away our sins. If a person has had an abortion or been a part of that industry, forgiveness is available if he or she repents, turns from the sin, and obeys the gospel.

When we teach the _____ , we must share that repentance is essential, and God's forgiveness is the good news!

5. Confessing sin, acknowledging what we have done against God's will, allows us to feel godly sorrow and repent, and to make lasting change in our lives. We accept God's gift of grace that removes the guilt of sin. Christians often mourn and feel grief over their past actions. Women who regret an abortion are bullied into silence by the abortion industry. Yet grieving is needed by women and others who repent over abortion. Paul wrote about being the chief of sinners for zealous persecution and even execution of Christians before his conversion. He held himself up as an example of the power of Christ's saving grace.

Complete 1 Timothy 1:15 from the New King James Version,
"This is a faithful saying and worthy of all acceptance, that Christ Jesus

Be Obedient

came into the world to _____
_____, of whom I am chief."[208]

6. False Teaching: Some people teach that **'the end justifies the means'** (i.e., an outcome perceived as beneficial justifies any evil employed to accomplish it) and that **'might makes right'** (i.e., those with power take precedence over those without it). Which of these false premises do you hear most often behind these pro-abortion arguments?

   a) "It is my body[209]. I should have the right to decide if or when I want to give birth."
   b) "Others (the state, voters, the father of a baby, doctors, God, etc.) should have no say in what a woman does with her own body."
   c) "I cannot do this. I cannot bear the humiliation of being pregnant or take care of another person. I am not ready to be a parent."
   d) "A woman's mental-health, career plans, financial hardships, health, etc. could be negatively affected, so aborting a fetus should be her decision."
   e) "Equality of the sexes can only be achieved if women have the same sexual freedom as men and are as free from undesired consequences as men."
   f) "Abortion reduces the birthrate in communities with historically high adolescent crime rates (stance akin to genocide in its stated intent and effect)."
   g) "Fetal tissues are valuable (highly profitable) in medical research, certain medical procedures, saving some lives, and trying to cure paralysis. Surely, benefitting a living person deserves consideration above that of a fetus."
   h) "Pro-Choice" or "Women's Health" vs. "Anti-Abortion"

7. Match each Scripture to the human reasoning (a-h) that it refutes.

   I. "Behold, **children are a heritage from the LORD, The fruit of the womb is a reward**."[210]

   This refutes human reasoning in item(s) _____, because

II. *"Thus says the L*ORD*, your Redeemer,*
   *And **He who formed you from the womb**:*
   "I am the Lord, who makes all things,
   Who stretches out the heavens all alone,
   ***Who spreads abroad the earth by Myself;**"*[211]

This refutes human reasoning in item(s) _____ , because

III. ***"Know that the LORD, He is God;***
   It is He who has made us, and not we ourselves;
   We are His people and the sheep of His pasture." [212]

This refutes human reasoning in item(s) _____ , because

IV. *"Did not He who made me in the womb make them? **Did not the same One fashion us in the womb?**"*[213]

This refutes human reasoning in item(s)_____ , because

V. ***"You shall not murder."***[214]

This refutes human reasoning in item(s)_____ , because

VI. *"Come now, you who say, "Today or tomorrow we will travel to such and such a city and spend a year there, and engage in business and make a profit." Yet you who do not know what your life will be like tomorrow. For you are just a vapor that appears for a little while and then vanishes away. **Instead you ought to say, "If the Lord wills, we will live and do this or that." But as it si you boast in your arrogance; all such boasting is evil. So for the one who knows the right thing to do and does not do it, for him it is sin."***[215]

This refutes human reasoning in item(s)_____ , because

Be Obedient

VII. *"Let nothing be done through selfish ambition or conceit, but in lowliness of mind **let each esteem others better than himself**. Let each of you look out not only for his own interests, but also for the interests of others."*[216]

This refutes human reasoning in item(s)_____, because

VIII. *"Or do you not know that **your body is the temple of the Holy Spirit** who is in you, whom you have from God, and **you are not your own? For you were bought at a price**; therefore glorify God in your body and in your spirit, which are God's."*[217]

This refutes human reasoning in item(s)_____, because

IX. *"**Flee sexual immorality**. Every sin that a man does is outside the body, but he who commits sexual immorality sins against his own body. Or do you not know that **your body is the temple of the Holy Spirit who is in you, whom you have from God, and you are not your own?**"*[218]

This refutes human reasoning in item(s)_____, because

X. *"Yet hear now, O Jacob My servant, And Israel whom I have chosen. **Thus says the Lord who made you And formed you from the womb**, who will help you:"*[219]

This refutes human reasoning in item(s)_____, because

XI. *"Then the word of the Lord came to me, saying: "**Before I formed you in the womb I knew you; Before you were born I sanctified you; I ordained you a prophet to the nations**."*[220]

This refutes human reasoning in item(s)_____, because

XII. *"Nevertheless, **because of sexual immorality, let each man have his own wife, and let each woman have her own husband**. Let the husband render to his wife the affection due her, and likewise also the wife to her husband. The **wife does not have authority over her own body, but the husband does. And likewise the husband does not have authority over his own body, but the wife does**. Do not deprive one another except with consent for a time, that you may give yourselves to fasting and prayer; and come together again so that Satan does not tempt you because of your lack of self-control."*[221]

This refutes human reasoning in item(s)_____ , because

Note: If you or someone you know has chosen to have an abortion, you need to know that God can forgive any sin if we are in Christ, confess, and repent of the sin. If you or someone you know is considering abortion, you need to know that God can bring blessings from difficult situations, including an unexpected baby. Please, do not let fear, pride, or social pressure lead you into sin. A woman does not know what the Lord can do with her life or the life of her child when she chooses to trust and obey God. The Lord's church can be a source of encouragement and assistance. His Word and Christian teachers can strengthen us to look beyond self and glorify our Father in heaven in all we do.

CALL TO ACTION

Support care for children who have been orphaned with funds and your time.

Help Christian families pay for adoptions.

Offer help to foster families with funds and your time.

Adopt or provide foster care if you are able. Befriend and encourage those who need you.

SONG AND PSALM

TRUST AND OBEY

PSALM 119:97-105
"Oh, how I love Your law!
    It is my meditation all the day.
You, through Your commandments,
    make me wiser than my enemies;
    For they are ever with me.
I have more understanding than all my teachers,
    For Your testimonies are my meditation.
I understand more than the ancients,
    Because I keep Your precepts.
I have restrained my feet from every evil way,
    That I may keep Your word.
I have not departed from Your judgments,
    For You Yourself have taught me.
How sweet are Your words to my taste,
    Sweeter than honey to my mouth!
Through Your precepts I get understanding;
    Therefore I hate every false way.
Your word is a lamp to my feet
    And a light to my path."[222]

SUGGESTED TOPIC FOR PRAYER

Pray for grace to be obedient in human relationships as God asks of us. Ask for wisdom to trust God's will above our own. Pray for deliverance of those being tempted by fornication and adultery. Ask God to help you be chaste, never allowing your desires to cause you or someone else to sin. Pray for those being enslaved by sex trade and those being abused, especially children.

BE KEEPERS

UNIT TWO

BE KEEPERS AT HOME

"That they may teach the young women to be sober, to love their husbands, to love their children, To be discreet, chaste, keepers at home, good, obedient to their own husbands, that the word of God be not blasphemed."

Titus 2:4–5, KJV

UNIT TWO INTRODUCTION

BE KEEPERS AT HOME

Lessons 5-7 teach about the great wisdom of God's plan for us as wives, mothers, and keepers of our homes. Our Creator established the home as the foundational unit of society. During His earthly ministry, Jesus taught that from the beginning, God intended one man and one woman to be joined in marriage for life. Titus 2:4-5 encourages mature Christian women to teach younger women about their responsibilities in marriage and the family.

In marriage, God created the wife to be a suitable helper for her husband. In the family, God gave women the biological role of childbearing and the responsibility of keeping the home. Because Eve allowed herself to be deceived, a wife's role is to submit to her husband as the head of their household. Submission in marriage is not a demeaning role but reflects the relationship of the church to Jesus Christ!

As foretold in Eden, salvation came from the Seed of woman. Clearly declaring that Christ was Immanuel, God incarnate, Jesus was born of a virgin with God as His Father in a miraculous conception like no other. Jesus is God's only begotten Son. Women and men can have salvation only in Jesus Christ who being God had to be born into a human body to live and die to redeem us. The Savior became incarnate through Mary's childbearing. All glory belongs to God who purposed before the foundation of the world to thus redeem us to Himself.

Our family relationships reflect the relationship we can have with our God. The husband's leadership is to be loving, like Christ's sacrificial love for the church. Children are to be obedient to parents, as we are to be obedient to our Heavenly Father and as Jesus did the will of the Father. Parents are to love their children, teach them God's Word, and diligently provide discipline. The family, church, and community flourish when the home is structured as God intends. When sin enters and God's commands are ignored, the family, church, and community suffer.

Women and men who obey the gospel are saved without bias in Jesus, but our roles in the church are not the same. Though women cannot preach to men, nor serve as elders or deacons, we have important work to do in the church. Our homes allow us to extend hospitality, not for social status, but to show the love of God to others. When we submit to God's will, we please God and extend His blessings to our marriage, family, and His church.

LESSON 5

BE GODLY WIVES

*"Who can find a virtuous wife?
For her worth is far above rubies.
The heart of her husband safely trusts her
So he will have no lack of gain.
She does him good and not evil All the days of her life.
... Charm is deceitful, and beauty is passing,
But a woman who fears the LORD,
she shall be praised."*

Proverbs 31:10-12, 30

Young men and women, who are serious about their faith, usually search for a Christian spouse. Christian parents want each of their children to find a godly mate. They want their children to prepare diligently to be the husband or wife that God expects them to be. Inside marriage, a shared faith can bring peace and purpose to a home. Christian women, your worth was not fixed when your husband proposed. We can grow more precious to our husbands and God as we gain in Christian virtues!

 BEE-ATTITUDE: WORK TOGETHER
Honeybees work together. Their cooperation accomplishes tasks that solitary bees can never do. As a colony, they build the honeycomb, gather nectar

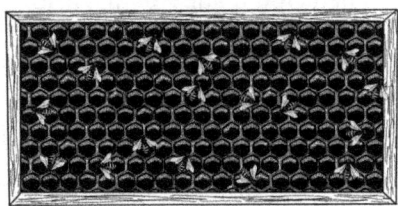

and pollen, and store away honey. As a colony, they care for the young, feed the queen, and clean the hive. Honeybees can fan with their wings to cool or use their active body heat to regulate the hive's temperature to 92°F even in cold weather. Most bee behavior is instinctive, but depositing honey in the comb and fanning it to evaporate its water content is learned behavior that older bees teach younger bees. A single bee will only produce 1/12 teaspoon of honey, but a healthy hive produces enough honey to fill a five-gallon bucket each year!

Just as God provided a plan for honeybees, God established the human family. He created us to need one another. Genesis' inspired account of creation also holds God's plan for the interdependence of husband and wife:

- Man does not need to be alone.[223]
- No animal is an adequate companion.[224]
- Woman was formed from the rib of man to be a suitable helper for him.[225]
- God gave man work to do and commanded him to do His will.[226]
- God's family plan provides for a husband and wife to be joined as one flesh and raise children together.[227]
- Jesus Christ confirmed that from the beginning God has joined a man and woman in marriage for life.[228]

We can learn how to treat others, including our spouse, from God's Word and from godly examples. The Bible teaches that mature Christian women are to teach younger women to love their husbands and children, submit to their husband's leadership, and care for the home.[229] This lesson focuses on loving our husbands, encouraging their leadership, and working together to create a home that glorifies God.

A HELP MEET FOR HIM

When God made Adam, He formed Him from the dust of the ground, but in the image of God. Then, our loving Father breathed into man's nostrils the breath of life, making him a living soul. God planted a garden in Eden with beautiful trees that were good for food and placed Adam there with the responsibility to tend it. God gave Adam good gifts. In that garden was the Tree of the Knowledge of Good and Evil. God told Adam not to eat of it, *"for in the day you eat of it, you will surely die."*[230]

Eating of the tree was acting against God's will and therefore sin. Even before creation, God had a plan for redeeming man from sin, though it would be self-sacrifice. John says that Christ as the Word was with God at creation and that everything was created through Him.[231] We are told that Christ was foreordained to be our Savior before the foundation of the world.[232] What a precious son Adam was to God!

God knew that man needed woman but taught Adam this by giving him the task of naming all the cattle, birds, and beasts. One-by-one God brought them to Adam to name, but when the great task was complete, no suitable helper had been found. God put Adam to sleep, removed a rib from his side, and formed woman from that rib. God brought her to Adam who welcomed her as *"bone of my bone and flesh of my flesh,"* establishing from the beginning that marriage is the unity of man and wife joined by God to be one flesh.[233]

God's beautiful ideal of a relationship between a husband and wife is that they work together to do His will, become one flesh, put one another's needs before their own, raise God- fearing children and grandchildren, and depend on their family as they advance in years. God did not create us to be alone. Marriage is God's metaphor for His relationship with His people, Israel, under the Old Law and the relationship of Christ to the church under the New Testament.[234] Our God created man and woman suited for a lifelong monogamous marriage.[235] Marriage was always intended for one man and one woman. Similarly, God is a jealous God.[236] There is no place for idolatry or sin in our relationship with Him. The husband-and-wife relationship is found in every civilization because it is what we are created to be.

LOVE YOUR HUSBAND

Isn't it wonderful when we are eager to do God's commands, like **love your husband**! Romantic spaghetti dinners, decorating your first apartment, anticipating your first baby ... all wonderful things to share. Loving our husbands means budgeting finite funds, handling disagreements with humility, and making compromises that put the other person ahead of yourself. Love elevates common chores like cleaning bathrooms, doing loads of laundry, and mowing lawns. Love illuminates the joy in putting self aside to do what your spouse or family needs.

Most Christian wives want to work alongside their husbands through the difficulties of life, knowing that trials will come. Marriage is rewarding when both people are steadfast sources of strength for one another. Some of the best advice I have heard offered to newlyweds is good for every marriage: Pray together, daily. Find joy in simple things. Say thank you to each other every chance you get. Do kind things for one another. Leave little notes or send uplifting text messages. Remember that a soft answer turns away wrath.[237] Love may be tried in the furnace when dealing with financial stress, unemployment, extended illnesses, loss of a child, or living with long-term disabilities. Love is hard work, but worthwhile.

Sometimes love is lonely work. Even when our husbands seem unlovable, we do the work of a wife as unto God and He will reward it. Real love is always God's work.

Sisters, put aside all the world's notions about marriage and relationships – everything rosy and sordid that has spilled out of Hollywood, Orlando, New York, and Nashville. Most media promote covetousness, lies, vanity, pride, fornication, selfishness, gossip, resentment, violence, lust, and infatuation in place of love.[238] These ideas come from the enemy.

Perhaps you have memorized 1 Corinthians 13 for its definition of love or charity, depending on the Bible translation you use. The Greek word being translated is *agape*, a verb for *acting to benefit another person*. It is given as the only worthy basis for our actions.[239] Jesus commands that we love one another.[240] The Holy Spirit defines what love is and is not.[241] God the Father, Son, and Holy Spirit are love.[242] Consider what these passages suggests for your life as we study three examples of a wife's love in Scripture.[243]

RUTH AND BOAZ

Love is longsuffering, kind. 'Never envious, prideful, vain, rude, or selfish.[244]

The Book of Ruth holds a precious love story of two God-fearing people who came together in marriage and became a part of the lineage of Jesus Christ. Ruth was a young Moabite widow who chose to remain faithful to her Jewish mother-in-law rather than look for a husband among her own pagan nation. Ruth's kindness and character were apparent to all as she humbly set out to glean the barley fields of Bethlehem to feed Naomi and herself. Boaz was a wealthy relative of the family who noted Ruth's conduct and encouraged her to glean in his fields. Naomi recognized God's providence at work and all of Bethlehem rejoiced when they married and later when their son, Obed, was born. Obed's son was Jesse. Jesse's son was David. Through the descendants of King David was born the promised Savior, Jesus Christ.[245]

When we love our husbands, we are longsuffering. Patience allows room for our will to be set aside so God's will can be done. Loving our husbands is being kind and caring about their needs and feelings. When we love our husbands, we build their confidence. We encourage their faith in God. We delight in their well-being.

Love is not envious of others, and covetousness is idolatry.[246] When we love our husbands, we do not push for material things or social status. Love is not prideful or vain.[247] When we love our husbands, we do not use them to establish prestige or press them toward achievements that require moral compromise. Loving your husband means you are not rude or selfish.

Ruth was such a person and showed her character in her roles as a daughter-in-law, wife, and mother. Her influence likely extended to the rearing of her great-grandson, David, who wrote beautiful psalms of faith as he tended sheep in the pastures of Bethlehem. Her own words of commitment to Naomi have inspired others for over 3,000 years. Many brides have recited them to their husbands at the altar,

> *"Entreat me not to leave you,*
> *Or to turn back from following after you;*
> *For wherever you go, I will go;*
> *And wherever you lodge, I will lodge;*
> *Your people shall be my people,*
> *And your God, my God. Where you die,*
> *I will die, And there will I be buried.*
> *The LORD do so to me, and more also,*
> *If anything but death parts you and me."*[248]

MICHAL AND ABIGAIL, WIVES OF DAVID

> Love ... is not provoked, thinks no evil, and does not rejoice in iniquity.[249]

The Holy Spirit inspired Paul to write that "love is not provoked, thinks no evil, and does not rejoice in iniquity." We can see a non-example and an example of these attributes of love in two of David's wives.[250] Michal was the younger daughter of King Saul, whom he gave to David hoping to ensnare him.

At first, Michal loved David, even deceiving her father when he repeatedly sought to kill her husband. Her father then gave her as a wife to another man, but David demanded her return to him after Saul's death. War arose between the house of Saul and the house of David. After a miraculous victory over the Philistines when David was returning from battle, the Scriptures say, "Michal, Saul's daughter, looked through a window and saw King David leaping and whirling before the LORD; and she despised him in her heart."[251]

Michal's words of rebuke were provoked by pride, attributed evil intentions to David's actions, and rejoiced in the iniquity of rebellion against her husband's kingship. David's reply suggests her loyalties were to Saul's house instead of King David whom God had anointed over Israel. The consequence was that Michal bore no children to link her father's house to the house of King David.

> "then David returned to bless his household. And Michal the daughter of Saul came out to meet David, and said, "How glorious was the king of Israel today, uncovering himself today in the eyes of the maids of his servants, as one of the base fellows shamelessly uncovers himself!"
>
> So David said to Michal, "It was before the LORD, who chose me instead of your father and all his house, to appoint me ruler over the people of the LORD, over Israel. Therefore I will play music before the LORD. And I will be even more undignified than this, and will be humble in my own sight. But as for the maidservants of whom you have spoken, by them I will be held in honor."

Therefore Michal the daughter of Saul had no children to the day of her death." [252]

In contrast, Abigail was first married to Nabal, a wealthy but foolish man who refused food for David's troops even after they had protected his flocks in the wilderness of Carmel. Nabal acted as if he did not know David. Nabal's herdsmen and servants knew David and took word of Nabal's offence to his wife. Abigail realized the gravity of the situation, knowing even that David had been anointed to be king of Israel. Abigail's loving charity was apparent in her immediate response to save her household.[253]

Abigail did not join Nabal in his evil thoughts or revel in his iniquity. She did not mock him, either. Instead, she took action to save others. She had servants gather generous provisions for David's men, then rode ahead to meet the 300 armed men David was bringing toward Nabal. Abigail bowed humbly before David, offered to bear her husband's reproach, and begged David not to allow Nabal's foolishness to provoke him to sin against God. David praised God for sending Abigail to meet him and keep him from taking vengeance into his own hands.

Abigail was not provoked to act against her husband but risked her own life to protect their household. She returned home to find Nabal drunk and feasting. The next morning when he was sober, she told him all that had transpired. Scripture says that his heart died within him, and he became like stone. Then after about 10 days, the Lord struck Nabal, and he died. When David learned of his death, he sent for Abigail to be his wife.

If we love our husbands, there are things we do not do. We are not provoked to do wrong against them. Neither are we provoked by them to harm others. We do not entertain covetous or vengeful thoughts, because evil thoughts lead to sinful words and actions. We do not participate with our husbands in sinful activities. We do not rejoice in iniquity, immoral, and unjust behaviors that exploit other people.

AQUILA AND PRISCILLA

Love . . . rejoices in the truth; bears all things, believes all things, hopes all things, endures all things. Love never fails.[254]

As the apostle Paul established churches throughout the Roman Empire where the Jews had immigrated, he usually began teaching the gospel in their synagogues. At Corinth, Paul met and worked with a Jew named Aquila and his wife, Priscilla, who were also tentmakers.[255] The couple had just come to Corinth because Claudius had commanded all Jews to leave Rome. The couple's names are always mentioned together in Scripture. Here they were enduring a milder persecution.

They believed Paul's teaching and rejoiced in truth, becoming obedient to the gospel, and taking hold of the hope that is in Christ. Together they took the eloquent preacher Apollos aside at Ephesus and taught him of Christ, for he only knew John's baptism.[256] Together, they accompanied Paul on a mission trip into Syria, bearing the threat of unbelieving Jews. The church met in their home.[257] Paul wrote that Priscilla and Aquila had risked their own necks to save his life.[258] All the churches of the Gentiles thanked God for them along with Paul.

What a beautiful example of a Christian marriage we see in Aquila and Priscilla! Both rejoiced in truth, in the faith, shared hope in Christ, and endured hardship. They worked together making tents and doing the work of the church. Like them, loving wives work with our husbands to provide for our families. Like them, we can do Bible studies together to bring others to Christ. Like them, we can open our homes to the church. We have brothers and sisters who face persecutions and execution for their faith in Christ; we may be called upon to do the same. The New Testament says nothing of the end of Aquila and Priscilla's lives, but we do know the eternal home for which they hoped and that love never fails. What greater goal could a family hold than to share eternal life?

GOD'S PLAN FOR HUSBANDS AND WIVES

Good leaders have the responsibility to make decisions and act with others' best interest in mind. Good followers respect those in authority, assume the responsibilities delegated to them, work toward the common goals, and encourage their leaders through difficulties. Moses, Joshua, Paul, and Christ all called for God's people to follow them as they followed God. When they did so, the nation flourished. When the people of Israel followed false gods and did their own will, the nation suffered. This happens in the home as well.

When husbands and wives are in subjection to Christ, their marriage is strengthened. Only in Christ can a marriage be all that God intended it to be. When the husband loves and cares for his wife, and the wife loves and submits to her husband, their relationship with God can also be stronger.[259] *"Wives, submit to your own husbands,"* is God's command.[260] A wife who is in subjection respects and encourages her husband's faith in the Lord, security in her love, and standing in the community.[261] Husbands and wives who treat each other with genuine care and respect, teach their children to love and respect their parents. They show them how to love and care for their own families as adults.

It isn't always easy to set aside our will in marriage, but it is parallel to what we should do for God. We must set aside our will to do God's will. Scripture says that although Jesus was the Son of God, He learned obedience. Jesus submitted to God with every lesson He taught, every miracle He performed, every apostle He chose. In death, he submitted to His Father as God's sacrificial Lamb to redeem us. The result is that God is glorified, we have the hope of salvation, and the resurrected Jesus Christ reigns in heaven.[262]

God's command is not a license for men to abuse authority but confers responsibility within the relationship. The wife submits to the husband, and children submit to their parents.[263] The wife submits to her husband, and both are in submission to Christ as His church. Christ has been given authority over all things but will return them to God the Father at the day of judgment. Wives who obey bring glory to God. When we do not do His will, we bring reproach upon the church for whom Christ died.[264] Now, you know the gravity of your responsibility. Don't miss the blessings that come from living like Christ, doing God's will!

Just as there are far-reaching consequences when women refuse to submit to the husband's leadership in the home, there are lasting problems when men resent their wives, misuse their authority, neglect, or selfishly dominate the family. Unresolved arguments inhibit our prayers. Sin in a marriage of Christians harms the church. Self-centeredness hurts the spouse we have vowed to love. Continual conflict between the husband

and wife damages the spiritual and mental health of everyone in the household. As the home is eroded, so is society. When homes and marriages are not lived as God directs, society sees increases in adultery, domestic abuse, divorce, depression, mental illness, juvenile crime, alcoholism, drug abuse, suicide, pornography, sexual promiscuity, homosexuality, feminism, abortion, cohabitation without marriage, gambling, and every evil under the sun. It is happening all around the globe in this generation as it has before the fall of many earthly kingdoms.

Let's not pretend that all women are sugar and spice and everything nice. The scriptures are clear that wickedness is to be found in many women. Even Christian women must guard against feminist-promoted negativity toward men. When our husbands are successful, we must guard against snobbish pride. When they suffer setbacks, we must guard against resentment.

Always, we must keep our hearts from covetousness, never trusting material possessions or wealth instead of God. These are idolatry.

When the beloved patriarch, Job, lost all his children and his wealth in a single day at the whim of the devil, his wife suffered the same loss. However, at one point it seems that she became bitter toward God while Job refused to do so. There are 16 chapters in the book of Job dedicated to the reasoning of his friends as they debated whether Job had sinned against God, but only two painful verses are given to her angry words.

When God allowed the devil to bring boils on Job from head to foot, his wife said, *"Do you still hold fast to your integrity? Curse God and die!"*[265] You can hear the deep disappointment in his reply, *"You speak as one of the foolish women speaks. Shall we indeed accept good from God, and shall we not accept adversity?"*[266] When our husbands endure the pain of this fallen world, let us never speak words of discouragement as one of the foolish women. If we do, we are allowing the evil one to use us as a weapon against our own husband. Instead, let us invite God to make our homes safe havens of joy and bastions of faith.

GOD'S WORDS TO HUSBANDS AND WIVES

"He who finds a wife finds a good thing,
And obtains favor from the Lord."[267]

"Who can find a virtuous wife?
For her worth is far above rubies.
The heart of her husband safely trusts her;
So he will have no lack of gain. She does
him good and not evil All the days of her life."
'Charm is deceitful and beauty is passing,
But a woman who fears the Lord, She shall
be praised.'"[268]

"A foolish son is the ruin of his father, And
the contentions of a wife are a continual
dripping."[269]

"Wives, submit to your own husbands,
as is fitting in the Lord.

Husbands, love your wives and do not be
bitter toward them.

Children, obey your parents in all things,
for this is well pleasing to the Lord.

Fathers, do not provoke your children,
lest they become discouraged.

... And whatever you do, do it heartily,
as to the Lord and not to men,
knowing that from the Lord you will
receive the reward of the inheritance;
for you serve the Lord Christ.

But he who does wrong will be repaid
for what he has done, and there is no
partiality." "But if anyone does not provide
for his own, and especially for those of his
household, he has denied the faith and is
worse than an unbeliever."[270]

"Let nothing be done through selfish ambition or conceit, but in lowliness of mind let each esteem others better than himself.[271]

"Husbands, likewise, dwell with them with understanding, giving honor to the wife, as to the weaker vessel, and as being heirs together of the grace of life, that your prayers may not be hindered."[272]

Note the parallels between God's plan for marriage and His plan for the church in Ephesians 5.

GOD'S PLAN FOR MARRIAGE AND THE CHURCH

Wives, <u>submit</u> to your own husbands, <u>as to the Lord</u>.

For the husband is <u>head</u> of the wife, <u>as also Christ is head</u> of the church; and He is the <u>Savior</u> of the <u>body</u>.

Therefore, just as the church is subject to Christ, so let the wives be to their own husbands in everything.

Husbands, love your wives, just as Christ also loved the church and gave Himself for her, that He might sanctify and cleanse her with the washing of water by the word, that He might present her to Himself a glorious church, not having spot or wrinkle or any such thing, but that she should be holy and without blemish.

So husbands ought to love their own wives as their own bodies; he who loves his wife loves himself. For no one ever hated his own flesh, but nourishes and cherishes it, just as the Lord does the church.

For we are members of His body, of His flesh and of His bones.

For this reason a man shall leave his father and mother and be joined to his wife, and the two shall become one flesh.

Describe any parallels in the text

> This is a great mystery, but I speak concerning Christ and the church. Nevertheless let each one of you in particular so love his own wife as himself, and let the wife see that she respects her husband."[273]

WHAT GOD'S WORD SAYS OF INTIMACY

The godly wife provides support in a partnership with her husband. It is God's plan and to His glory that a wife accepts her husband's leadership in their home. God also planned for marriage to provide romantic love exclusively and selflessly for both the husband and wife. Just as our God is a jealous God who does not tolerate infidelity and idolatry in our relationship with Him, He commands fidelity in marriage.[274] From the beginning, God intended to permanently bond husband and wife, male and female.

> *"Therefore a man shall leave his father and mother and be joined to his wife, and they shall become one flesh. And they were both naked, the man and his wife, and were not ashamed."*[275]

Passion belongs in marriage and strengthens it.

> *"Your lips, O my spouse,*
> *Drip as the honeycomb;*
> *Honey and milk are under your tongue;*
> *And the fragrance of your garments*
> *Is like the fragrance of Lebanon."*[276]

Sexual relations are not to be withheld. Marriage gives the spouse the right to expect physical affection. Scripture only gives sexual abstinence during a period of fasting and prayer as a reason to refuse one another. Seeking sex outside marriage is sinful.

> *"Let the husband render to his wife the affection due her, and likewise also the wife to her husband. The wife does not have authority over her own body, but the husband does. And likewise the husband does not have authority over his own body, but the wife does.*

Do not deprive one another except with consent for a time, that you may give yourselves to fasting and prayer; and come together again so that Satan does not tempt you because of your lack of self-control" (1 Corinthians 7:3-5).

WIFE, WIDOW, OR SINGLE?

Christianity is unlike the world in many, many ways. God's plan for the family is perfect, but every aspect is under attack by the devil, as is every truth. For many in the world, sexual relations are casual; partners may be innumerable; sexual perversions are tolerated, celebrated, and vaguely attributed to genetics; co-habitation without marriage is prevalent; abortion is a multi-billion-dollar industry;[277] every imaginable living situation is deemed a family; many parents do not support, teach, discipline, or love their children; divorce is more common than a 25th anniversary;[278] and domestic abuse is commonplace. Even gender is questioned. Christians must not conform to the world.[279]

ARE YOU A CHRISTIAN WIFE?

Live as God commands and enjoy the blessings it brings. Paul described the life of a Christian widow whom the church could support as the wife of one man, known for raising children, lodging strangers, washing the saints' feet, relieving the afflicted, and diligently following every good work. He also wrote that the wife of a deacon or elder should be reverent, not a slanderer, temperate, and faithful in all things.[280] We should all strive to be such a person. Be active in the work of the church. Do not think that God's work belongs to the men or only to older members of the congregation. Involve your children in the good works you do.

If you are married to a non-Christian, as a Christian wife you will still do God's will even if your husband does not. Christianity is your way of life. Live your life to please God. Don't beleaguer your husband about "going to church." Do not allow him to keep you from attending worship and Bible study. If he participates in sinful activities, do not join in these things.

Otherwise, you are to submit to your husband as you would to a Christian spouse. God's Word says you will best persuade your husband by setting a godly example and may even help save his soul![281]

ARE YOU A WIDOW?

Continue living like a Christian wife. Be active in the church, in prayer, and in teaching others. Be active in your family. Trust in God. Your example will benefit everyone around you. If you someday wish to date, date a Christian. If you remarry, marry a Christian.[282]

ARE YOU SINGLE AND WISH TO BE MARRIED?

Use your time in preparation for the role you seek, becoming the woman God commands you to be. When you are prepared to be a Christian wife, look for a Christian husband. Know your responsibility is to be his suitable helper, living as God's Word teaches. Treat one another with respect when you are dating and plan together to live in submission to Christ so your home can be a place of joy and blessing.

Do not wait to be married before being active in the work of the church. Young Christian women and men need to be active in the church of today, not waiting to be the church of tomorrow. All women can offer to go with others to visit those who are sick, shut-in, or in prison. Send cards of encouragement. Offer to help prepare or deliver meals. Participate in teaching or co-teaching children's classes with another woman. Sing at weddings and funerals.

Sing out with spirit and understanding. Participate in and/or support mission trips. Babysit while other families do church work. Take Bible courses. Attend gospel meetings. Do Bible studies with other women. Invite non-Christian friends to join you. Help with maintaining the church's building and grounds. Pray for those in need of healing, spiritual strengthening, or conversion. Pray for the elders, deacons, preachers, and mission workers. Pray for our nation, families, children, and the church worldwide. If you see someone who is not yet active, invite them to help in a work. If you don't know what to do, ask!

SEVEN-POINT DISCUSSION GUIDE

Use your Bibles to find the truth about each of the statements you hear in the world today. Write book, chapter, and verse for what Scripture says on each topic. Note what God's truth is on each lie being propagated by the devil.

1. False Teaching: Gender (being male or female) is just a human concept. Gender is fluid, changeable.[283]

2. False Teaching: Marriage can be between any two people who are in love.[284]

3. False Teaching: Divorce is understandable when people grow apart and are no longer compatible.[285]

4. False Teaching: Living together first is a great way to decide if you should marry a person.[286]

5. False Teaching: The Bible lets husbands treat their wives like property or slaves.[287]

6. False Teaching: The Bible permits (vs. records instances of) polygamy.

7. False Teaching: Women are belittled by traditional roles.

CALL TO ACTION

Openly discuss these issues with your friends in and outside the church. Remind others that there are truths defined by God and that the origin and ultimate outcome of such lies is evil.

"LOVE ONE ANOTHER"
"HUMBLE YOURSELVES IN THE SIGHT OF THE LORD"

SUGGESTED TOPICS FOR PRAZYER:

The prayers of a wife and mother are many. Pray to be a helper suited to your husband. Pray for God to bless you with understanding, so you will know how to be in subjection to God's glory. Pray for wisdom and patience. Pray for deliverance from covetousness and pride. Pray for eyes that see opportunities to demonstrate your love for your husband and encourage him in his walk with God. Pray for opportunities to work together for the sake of the gospel and family.

LESSON 6

BE LOVING MOTHERS

*"I have no greater joy than to hear
that my children walk in truth."*

3 John 1:4

The apostle John lived longer than his peers. He suffered much persecution as he spread the gospel message, yet God preserved his life. The Gospel According to John was the last of the four Gospel accounts and is structured differently. He humbly calls himself the apostle whom Jesus loved or that apostle. He gave us the account of Jesus' teaching Nicodemus when our Lord revealed, *"For God so loved the world that He gave His only begotten Son, that whoever believes in Him should not perish but have everlasting life."*[288] John emphasized Christ's command that we are to love one another as He loved us in his Gospel and his three letters to churches. My children, as used in 3 John 1:4 (above), is John's term of endearment for those to whom he had brought to Christ. Here we borrow His words, for Christian mothers share his great desire that those we love will remain faithful to our Lord Jesus.

BEE-ATTITUDE: LOVE YOUR CHILDREN
Honeybees live in nurturing colonies, unlike 90% of the world's bees, which are solitary.

a) Workers build the cells of the honeycomb where the queen bee deposits eggs. It takes about three days for larvae to hatch.
b) Workers, called brood nurses, mix a body secretion with pollen and honey to make bee bread that they continually feed to larvae for six days.
c) Then the worker bees seal each cell with wax, and the well-fed larvae enter the pupae stage of metamorphosis.
d) In 10 days, new worker bees emerge.
e) A bee's first job is to clean her own cell to be reused for honey or hatching.
f) For the first three weeks of life, worker bees' responsibilities are inside the hive: removing dead bees, feeding bee larvae, making wax for the honeycomb, and guarding the hive entrance.
g) Around 22 days of age, worker bees begin to serve as field bees, venturing increasing distances from the hive to gather pollen and nectar.

Motherhood has parallels to the honeybees' rearing of young. From conception, a godly mother provides her children proper physical, social, and spiritual nourishment in a safe, clean home. Her instruction, guidance, and discipline help prepare children to assume increasing responsibilities. As they mature, godly nurturing helps our sons and daughters gain the knowledge, skills, understanding, and character needed for independent living. Obviously, the command to *love your children* means to invest more than hugs and kisses. It takes disciplined, deliberate, dedicated parenting to raise a god-fearing person with the capacity to care for self and others.

This lesson will establish more of what love is in a family relationship, extending the previous chapter's focus on a godly wife's partnership, romantic love, and acceptance of her husband's leadership. This lesson is filled with Scriptures for you to read on your own time, thoroughly understanding how God has taught us to parent with love for our children.

GOD'S COMMANDS FOR LOVE IN THE FAMILY
What does God tell us about love? Titus 2:4-5 describes the character that older women should train younger women to have: pure, kind,

self-controlled, lovers of their husbands and children. The Greek word, *philoteknous*,[289] (translated as 'lovers of their children') is an adjective that describes a mother by her **ongoing care** for her children.

Indeed, **love** in Scripture is typically a **verb**, something we are **commanded to do**. We are to love God with all our hearts, minds, souls, (emotion, thought, and understanding) but also with all our strength (effort and action)![290] Loving our brethren was defined by Jesus as feeding, clothing, and visiting them when they are sick or in prison.[291] Loving our enemies is defined in context as doing good to them and lending without expecting repayment.[292] Much has been preached about wives' submission to their husbands, but loving your husband and children is part of obeying the second commandment!

GOD AS OUR FATHER

Many aspects of life on earth reflect things that are true spiritually. If we live according to God's Word, we come to understand more about our Heavenly Father and holiness. In God we learn of true love, repentance, forgiveness, peace, hope, and mercy. The first chapters of Genesis reveal that God is Creator of everything from the vast universe to the tiniest organism, and that He is our Creator. These scriptures record divine establishment of light and darkness, day and night, land and seas, seasons, genetic functions that preserve species, male and female genders, right and wrong, marriage, family, work, worshipping God according to His will, consequences for sin, sacrifice, forgiveness, and hope in Christ (the seed of woman). Creation itself was an act of love. In Eden we glimpse the delight of living in a home created by God the Father and in His presence.

In his rebellion against God, the devil lost the privilege of being in God's presence. Today, the devil's time is growing short, so he works hard to undermine all that God established, especially those truths recorded in Genesis. God created, so the devil proliferates atheistic theories of earth and man's origin. God's Word is truth, so the devil deals in deceit. God created us male and female, so the devil promotes gender-bending and homosexuality. God is our role model for parenting. Godly parents help others understand God as our Father, so the devil attacks marriage, family, and parenting. Yet God is able to keep us. His truth endures. Jesus Christ's death and resurrection deprived sin and death of their power. The choice is ours. The devil only has what people yield to him. If we believe and obey God, eternal life in can be ours in a place He has prepared for us.

Read again of creation and the lives of Adam and Eve in Genesis 2:1-5:5. Think about the example of parenting He is for us. God provided a universe of stars, earth for a home, the light of the sun by day, and moonlight by night. He gave Adam and Eve fruit trees for food and four rivers to nourish the garden He had planted as their home. He gave Adam purposeful work tending the garden and companionship in Eve. God spent time each evening the man and woman. He taught them to obey and warned them of the consequences of disobedience.

When they sinned, God followed through on His consequences, but did not stop caring for them or teaching them and their children. Yes, Adam worked and fought weeds to raise food to eat. Eve bore many children enduring the pain of childbirth, but she still glorified God for giving her children. They raised children to love God, love one another, know God's will, and offer sacrifice to Him. Their grandchildren began praying to God. All knew the hope of reconciliation that God promised in the Seed of woman, Christ whose sacrifice would take away their sins and ours.

What does a loving parent do according to Scripture? We imitate God's providence, love, teaching, companionship, guidance, constancy, discipline, and mercy. Take an hour for Bible study, and read the verses referenced for each aspect of parenting, below:

a) Respect that each child is a gift of God from conception.[293]
b) Provide shelter, food, and clothing.[294]
c) Diligently teach God's Word, the love of God, and the gospel to our children and grandchildren.[295]
d) Teach children to love others and choose good companions.[296]
e) Teach obedience of parents, obedience of God's commandments, and the value of disciple by a parent or by God.[297]
f) Diligently train and discipline children, without abuse.[298]
g) Teach responsibility.[299]
h) Teach the value of the home and God's plan for the family.[300]

i) Teach the danger of God's judgment and the consequences of sin.[301]
j) Model charity, mercy, faith, repentance, forgiveness, prayer, study of Scripture, obedience, and righteousness.[302]
k) Honor our parents and teach children to honor us as parents, even as adults. Honor is respect, obedience, and gifts of time, care, or financial care when needed.[303]
l) Encourage maturing in thought, actions, faith, and godliness. Celebrating the blessings that come from trusting God.[304]
m) Discourage foolishness, evil companions, pride, greed, materialism, anger, violence, envy, prejudice, and fear.[305]

SHAME

The word *shame* has become lost from the American vernacular. Shame is not removed from God's Word, and we can still suffer it in God's sight. It is to our shame when we fail to diligently train our children. Overindulgence is no more love than is neglect. Neglect is failing to feed, clothe, and educate a child. It is also neglect when a woman does not teach right from wrong, discipline, or God's Word. Far more than being a social embarrassment, the shame of failing to be a loving mother is that we have not treasured and developed the precious gift of a child, an eternal soul entrusted to us by God. Do not yield to social pressures to withhold religious training or leave your child's gender to question. If the lazy steward who buried a sum of money in the ground was worthy of being cast into outer darkness, what is just for a woman who will not be a loving mother to her child?[306]

Negligence is condemned in Proverbs 29:15, *"The rod and rebuke give wisdom, But a child left to himself brings shame to his mother."* Scripture warns that society suffers because of neglectful parenting, *"The people will be oppressed, Every one by another and every one by his neighbor; The child will be insolent toward the elder, And the base toward the honorable."*[307] Parenting is exhorting, admonishing, and giving charge to our children to walk worthy of God who calls you into His own kingdom and glory. Genesis does not address it, but as a parent, I can imagine how devastating it was for Adam and Eve to lose Abel at the hands of Cain, knowing that their own sin had brought death into God's good creation. Our children can bring great joy. They also bring great responsibility. Avoid shame and glorify God in your homes by having children's spiritual training take precedence.

GROWING IN FAVOR WITH GOD AND MAN

Loving your children is bringing them up to love and fear God. It is the best life you can offer a child.[308] Mothers and fathers must parent so that children develop into the person God wants them to be. Proverbs 20:11 says that *"Even a child is known by his deeds, whether what he does is pure and right."* If one is an obedient, kind-hearted four-year-old, those traits can be developed, so they will be responsible and good to others at ages 14, 24, and 40! A child that is being selfish or defiant needs models, teaching, and consequences to develop empathy, love, and the desire to obey.[309] Jesus wanted little children brought to Him. Loving your child certainly includes taking them to Bible classes and worship so they can learn the truths of God from infancy![310]

Scripture says the child, Samuel, the last of the Israel's judges, *"grew in stature, and in favor both with the Lord and men."*[311] Samuel was faithful to God throughout his life. Similarly, it was said of young Jesus, "And Jesus increased in wisdom and stature, and in favor with God and men."[312] This is stated in assurance that Jesus Christ was fully human and fully divine when He was incarnate (in the flesh). As Christian parents we hope for the same in our children, that they not only grow taller but gain wisdom, knowledge, strength, and spiritual maturity.

We need to give children the guidance, examples, and responsibilities that fit their age.

They must know God's truth to live uprightly and keep their hearts pure. Paul said that as he became a man, he *"put away childish things."*[313] Look for opportunities to acknowledge your sons' and daughters' growth and the evidence of their faith. Encourage them as they put away childish things. Teach them to be faithful to Christ from their youth up. What you value matters.

Remember, God the Father spoke from heaven at Jesus' submission to baptism, *"You are My beloved Son, in whom I am well pleased."*[314]

PARENTING GROWN CHILDREN

The Bible shares many true examples of parents' interactions with adult sons, yet the most powerful example for parenting young adults remains Jesus' vivid parable of the young man who squandered his inheritance in prodigal living. As we discussed earlier, the human father in Luke 16:11-32 represents God the Father. We are not told about the teaching the father had done as his boys grew into men, but it is implied when the son who went astray came to himself, he said, *'" How many of my father's hired servants have bread enough and to spare, and I perish with hunger! I will arise and go to my father, and will say to him, "Father, I have sinned against heaven and before you, and I am no longer worthy to be called your son. Make me like one of your hired servants."*[315] He had been taught right from wrong. His sense of responsibility was returning. He knew to respect his father. He understood that he had sinned and needed to repent and be forgiven. He also knew he could always go home. No doubt he had seen mercy, justice, and responsibility in the life his father lived as well as his teaching.

The father in the parable also addresses the older brother who is resentful and unforgiving. He does not ignore his inappropriate reaction to the celebration of the younger brother's return. He does not justify his son's resentment. He does not yield to the older son's anger or promise him a party. He teaches him to forgive and rejoice that his brother was restored. He helps him realize the severity of the situation, saying, *"your brother was dead and is alive again, and was lost and is found."*[316] The father was watching for both sons. He went out to meet each of them. He brought each of them home. He directed their attention to spiritual things that mattered and away from squandered money. The father was clear and firm, expecting righteousness from each son.

Sometimes mothers and fathers hesitate about parenting because society pushes for control in the lives of teenagers and young adults. These are vulnerable times for young people, even those from Christian homes. Many godless, ill-intentioned people seek to indoctrinate children contrary to their family values even in the elementary and preschool years. Society in mass media, social media, and school or college classrooms frequently mock strict morals and family traditions. Parents must always be vigilant. Previous generations talked of "sewing wild oats" and imagined that young people would later "settle down" into more conservative lifestyles. Whatever the generation, sin by any other name is still as deadly. Parents' yielding to such influence is abdicating responsibility for our sons and daughters and to our God. Prepare your families to defend against evil. Stand unabashedly against the wiles of the devil.[317]

My friends' parents in the 1970s said things like, "as long as you live under my roof, you will abide by my rules." Of course, my friends responded with, "I cannot wait to get out of this house." The rules and expectations in a Christian home do not originate from the strong will of a parent. They are not enforced by the economic necessity of a minor's dependence on parents' financial support. Instead, we teach our children what is right and wrong based on God's law and righteousness.[318] We train our children to obey whether anyone is looking and whether they are 8, 18, 38, or 88 years of age.[319] We teach them that they live all every moment of their lives in the sight of a Holy God. We teach them to obey God out of love, gratitude, and respectful fear.[320] We teach them to find purpose and delight in God's Word and His Way.[321]

As Christian parents, we must immerse our families in God's Word and warn them about the many ways the devil attempts to ensnare us.[322] Teach each child God's truth, so he or she can discern the lies of the devil. Do not be dissuaded by social pressures and compromise. See temptations for what they are, snares of the evil one. You have the God-given right and responsibility to teach and discipline your children.

Even adult sons and daughters living out of the home remain our responsibility. In 1 Samuel 3, when Eli's adult sons were sinning, God held Eli responsible for not restraining them. Parents and offspring do not answer for one another's sins, but we have a great responsibility to one another as Christians. We are commanded not to make another stumble.[323] We are compelled to try to save others when they fall into sin and restore them to the church.[324] We can humbly and lovingly address sin in one another's lives.[325] We are to go to those who offend and teach them the truth. If these are responsibilities to other Christians, how much more are we responsible for our own adult children? If failing to care for the physical needs of our relatives is worse in God's sight than being an infidel (unbeliever), can we excuse ourselves from responsibility for addressing the spiritual well-being of children just because they are 18 or 21?[326]

Help your children mature with a faith that endures by being consistent in attending worship and making God the head of your home. Talk about decision-making in the light of God's Word from the time your children are small. Help them resolve conflicts with siblings and peers based on scripture.[327] Teach them to pray before making decisions. Encourage Christian friendships and relationships with people of all ages in your congregation and family.

Our approach will be different to adult offspring, but we can fight for their souls when needed. Often that battle is fought on our knees in prayer. Throughout life, we must parent with the knowledge thar our sons and daughters will answer for their own sins before God.[328] Even faithful children need our encouragement in their walk of faith. We can help teach our grandchildren God's will and the gospel.[329] May you delight in doing God's will and be able to say of your own children what John said of those he had taught the gospel, *"I have no greater joy than to hear that my children walk in truth."*[330]

SEVEN-POINT DISCUSSION GUIDE

For each human doctrine below, give a pertinent Scripture reference, then write what it means for a woman to do to love her children as God commands.

1. False Teaching: Loving children means allowing them to do as they please.

    What is God's truth? Scripture:

2. False Teaching: Early religious training deprives children of the right to choose their own faith or beliefs.

    What is God's truth? Scripture:

3. False Teaching: Children should be allowed to choose their own gender.

    What is God's truth? Scripture:

4. False Teaching: Discipline is only punishment. All punishment is abuse.

   What is God's truth? Scripture:

5. False Teaching: Right and wrong do not exist. They are no absolute standards for human behavior, only cultural differences.

   What is God's truth? Scripture:

6. False Teachings: Life does not begin at conception. Unborn children are only masses of tissue, at most a fetus without human rights. Abortion is a right exercised by a woman over her own body.

   What is God's truth? Scripture:

7. False Teachings: It acceptable for men (or women) to choose to have children outside of marriage and/or choose not to support their children.

   What is God's truth? Scripture:

CALL TO ACTION

Work with your own children, in the Bible study program of your congregation, or in mission work. How? Pray without ceasing. Contribute your time. Contribute materials. Provide transportation. Host youth activities. Teach VBS, classes, or devotionals. Listen to children recite memory verses. Study and set a godly example. Welcome young families. Babysit so parents can be active in church work. Invite young people to come along as you do church work.

SONG AND PSALMS

"HOW SHALL THE YOUNG SECURE THEIR HEARTS?"

PSALM 127

A SONG OF ASCENTS. OF SOLOMON.
"Unless the LORD *builds the house,*
They labor in vain who build it;
Unless the LORD *guards the city,*
The watchman stays awake in vain.
It is vain for you to rise up early,
To sit up late,
To eat the bread of sorrows;
For so He gives His beloved sleep.

Behold, children are a heritage from the LORD,
The fruit of the womb is a reward.
Like arrows in the hand of a warrior,
So are the children of one's youth.
Happy is the man who has his quiver full of them;
They shall not be ashamed,
But shall speak with their enemies in the gate."[331]

PSALM 78:1-7
"Give ear, O my people, to my law;
Incline your ears to the words of my mouth.
I will open my mouth in a parable;
I will utter dark sayings of old,
Which we have heard and known,
And our fathers have told us.
We will not hide them from their children,
Telling to the generation to come the praises of the LORD,
And His strength and His wonderful works that He has done.
For He established a testimony in Jacob,

And appointed a law in Israel,
Which He commanded our fathers,
That they should make them known to their children;
That the generation to come might know them,
The children who would be born,
That they may arise and declare them to their children,
7 That they may set their hope in God,
And not forget the works of God,
But keep His commandments;" [332]

PSALM 34:11-14
"Come, you children, listen to me;
I will teach you the fear of the LORD.
Who is the man who desires life,
And loves many days, that he may see good?
Keep your tongue from evil,
And your lips from speaking deceit.
Depart from evil and do good;
Seek peace and pursue it.[333]

SUGGESTED TOPIC FOR PRAYER
Pray for wisdom to love your children and diligently seek His guidance in God's Word.

LESSON 7

BE HOSPITABLE HOMEMAKERS

"Therefore, as we have opportunity, let us do good to all, especially to those who are of the household of faith."

Galatians 6:10

The New Testament contains numerous examples of hospitality. Jesus did not choose to have material possession because He came to point us toward that which is spiritual, real, and eternal. He taught us not to trust in the transient things of this world, but to value what is eternal. What we have is to be shared, especially with our sisters and brothers in Christ who are enduring hardships. There is no need to fear doing without necessities, for our Father in heaven provides for our needs.

BEE-ATTITUDE: EXTEND HOSPITALITY

Honeybees certainly do not invite anyone into their hives! However, bees in their diligence produce far more honey than needed for their own use, 30-100 pounds per hive per year! People are among the beneficiaries of their abundance.

Sharing what we have is the lesson of hospitality that we will draw from the honeybee. Whatever

our material wealth, all we have is a gift from God and should be shared with others, to His glory, and with great love! What has God entrusted to you?

Under the Mosaic Law, widows who were destitute could live and work in the temple. When Joseph and Mary presented the infant Jesus at the temple, an aged widow named Anna was inspired to come in just as Simeon was blessing them. Anna gave thanks to the Lord and testified of Him to all who looked for redemption in Jerusalem. Luke tells us she had been a widow for 84 years, never leaving the temple, but serving God with fasting and prayer.[334]

As we discussed in lesson 6, Paul gave directions for the church to assume responsibility for caring only for a widow who had no family. He described the works she must be known for, "Do not let a widow under sixty years old be taken into the number, and not unless she has been the wife of one man, well reported for good works: if she has brought up children, if she has lodged strangers, if she has washed the saints' feet, if she has relieved the afflicted, if she has diligently followed every good work."[335] What a powerful portrait of a Christian woman!

Notice that most of the good works listed are acts of hospitality.

CAN YOU COOK?

Martha opened her home to Jesus and His apostles. She fed them and believed earnestly in the Lord. Her sister, Mary, was eager to hear Jesus' teaching. Perhaps you know of Martha asking Jesus to send Mary to help her serve. She was being hospitable, but had become focused on the wrong things, so Jesus said, *"Martha, Martha, you are worried and troubled about many things. But one thing is needed, and Mary has chosen that good part, which will not be taken away from her"* (Luke 10:41-42). When we open our homes to others, it should not be about entertaining, but about Christian fellowship.

When the church began and many were in Jerusalem, far from home, the church came together in a wonderful work of fellowship. Acts 2 says, *"Now all who believed were together, and had all things in common, and sold their possessions and goods, and divided them among all, as anyone had need. So continuing daily with one accord in the temple, and breaking bread from house to house, they ate their food with gladness and simplicity of heart, praising God and having favor with all the people. And the Lord added to the church daily those who were being saved."*[336]

Christ said, *"When you give a dinner or a supper, do not ask your friends, your brothers, your relatives, nor rich neighbors, lest they also invite you back, and you be repaid. But when you give a feast, invite the poor, the maimed, the lame, the blind. And you will be blessed, because they cannot repay you; for you shall be repaid at the resurrection of the just."*[337] Many times Christ encouraged His disciples to provide for those in need and lay up treasure in the heavens. Just two days before His arrest, Jesus taught His disciples about the judgment and declared that how we have cared for one another will determine our eternal destiny![338]

ARE YOU A LISTENER?

Martha's sister, Mary, was the listener. She hung on every word that Jesus said. Be equally hungry for His teachings. Study. Listen to teachers and sermons with an ear to what God's will is for your life. Pray for His guidance and then study, and His will be made known for your life. I am not suggesting something will be provided for you different than the gospel, but Jesus promised, *"Seek and you will find."*[339]

Some of the greatest gifts we can give are our time and attention. This is true for our spouse, our children, our brethren, and those we might hope to teach the gospel. Listening to learn about another person is important. When you do, you show that you value him or her. Teaching the truth in love is how we share the gospel. Ask questions to learn more about others. Show your love by listening and then offer God's Word to address their needs.

DO YOU SEW?

Peter raised Dorcas from the dead at Joppa.[340] The Scripture says she was *"full of good works and charitable deeds"* (Acts 9:36). When Dorcas died, the widows she had cared for were so distraught that they sent for the apostle. They met Peter weeping and holding garments she had made for them. Peter knelt in prayer, and the Lord allowed him to raise Dorcas from death. This became known and brought many in Joppa to believe in the Lord!

Perhaps you have other skills that can be employed to benefit others. You might install a new faucet in a few minutes for someone who cannot afford a plumber. You might mow a lawn, prepare a meal, share clothing, or watch children while their parents do other work for the church. You will not know where your influence ends because you serve the God who feeds 5,000 with five barley loaves and two small fish.[341] Proverbs 31:20 describes the worthy woman, *"She extends her hand to the poor, Yes, she reaches out her hands to the needy."*

DO YOU CARE FOR YOUR OWN?

When we are homemakers, our homes are a blessing we can share with others. God values the work we do raising our children, being a godly wife to our husbands, and inviting others into our homes. Often, we have a season of caring for an aging parent or in-law in our homes. This is also God's work.[342] Caring for our relatives is God's work and should be done with the same love and dedication to glorify God in doing His will. Paul wrote in 1 Timothy 5:4, *"But if any widow has children or grandchildren, let them first learn to show piety at home and to repay their parents; for this is good and acceptable before God."* If you are caring for aging, disabled, or chronically ill family members, do not forget to rely upon God. Be prayerful when it is not easy. Be patient. Do it as unto the Lord. For edification, talk often to other Christians who have done the same work. Always look for the joy.

Peter's mother-in-law lived with them. We are told of Jesus' healing her of a fever. The scripture says that when He touched her, the fever left, then she got up and served them. Jesus healed her completely. What does it say of the gratitude and attitude of the woman who immediately set about to provide hospitality?

Archaeological work between 1838-1982 has uncovered the likely ruins of Peter's little house in Capernaum[b] where hospitality was extended to Jesus, the apostles, and the early church. It is the oldest-known structure used for Christian worship. In the fifth century, a hexagonal chapel was built over part of the structure, but both were leveled along with the city of Capernaum by an earthquake in 746 A.D. as foretold by Christ.[343] Now fully excavated, only low rock walls of ruins remain beneath a modern cathedral with a glass floor (1990). Nonetheless, the souls who knew its hospitality and met there to worship are eternal!

---

[b] To view this archaeological image, please visit https://www.biblicalarchaeology.org/daily/biblical-sites-places/biblical-archaeology-sites/the-house-of-peter-the-home-of-jesus-in-capernaum/#:~:text=(This%20house%20of%20Peter%20was,to%20the%20first%20century%20B.C

Be Hospitable Homemakers

Hospitality continued to be a central theme of Christianity in Acts and throughout the writings of the apostles. Study and make notes in this passage from Romans.

ROMANS 12:9-13

Let love *be* without hypocrisy. Abhor what is evil. Cling to what is good. *Be* kindly affectionate to one another with brotherly love, in honor giving preference to one another; not lagging in diligence, fervent in spirit, serving the Lord; rejoicing in hope, patient in tribulation, continuing steadfastly in prayer; distributing to the needs of the saints, given to hospitality.

DO YOU HAVE WEALTH TO SHARE?

Lydia was a businesswoman in Philippi who sold expensive purple fabrics. She asked a favor of the apostles when they established the church there, offering her home as a place for them to stay. Though Lydia was likely wealthy, for Paul and his companions to accept her hospitality was an affirmation of the Gentiles' acceptance into Christ, for previously a Jewish person would not have entered any Gentile's home.

Also at Philippi, the church met in the house of Philemon. We learn much from the brief letter written by Paul and delivered by Onesimus, a runaway slave from Philemon's household. Onesimus had made his way to Rome and there became a Christian who cared for Paul. The journey from Rome to Philippi to deliver Paul's brief epistle was over 1,000 miles. In it, Paul thanked Philemon for his hospitality to the church, his expected acceptance of Onesimus, and for preparing Paul a guest room. The epistle of Philemon holds an important reminder that we owe our souls' salvation to those who teach us the gospel. In comparison, the wealth of this world is rubbish. Then and now some who open their homes to others put themselves at risk for arrest or persecution for the faith. We are stewards of our material blessings, charged with using our resources to God's glory and to care for one another.

DO YOU KNOW POVERTY?

It is not necessary to have money to please God. Paul called Onesimus his 'own heart' and expressed gratitude for all this enslaved man had done for him.[344] Anna served with fasting and prayer. Christ said that trusting in riches prevented many from entering heaven. Mark and Luke each tell of a widow whom Jesus observed putting two tiny copper coins into the temple treasury. He said she put in more than all the rich out of their abundance, because she gave all that she had.[345] Mary praised God for elevating those of low estate. In time of famine, God sent the prophet Elijah to the widow of Zarephath in Sidon, a woman who thought she was preparing her last meal. God can use all who trust in Him. When we are not preoccupied with things of this world, we can focus on things of God.

DON'T BUILD BIGGER BARNS, SHARE

Christians are to work as unto the Lord, to provide for our families and others, but not to love or trust in money. Once, when asked to settle a dispute about an inheritance, Jesus refused but told a parable of a man whose harvest was great. The man thought to store it up for himself, tearing down his barns to build greater ones. Jesus said that the man's soul was required of him that night and all his gain benefitted nothing. Jesus said it is covetousness to trust in the abundance of things we possess rather than being rich toward God. Do you have more than you need? Don't build a bigger barn. Look for ways to share with those who are in need and be rich toward God.

Hospitality is a way of loving one another. Paul said that if someone had been a thief before their conversion they must steal no more but, quite the opposite, work to have something to give to others who are in need.[346] The apostle John wrote, *"By this we know love, because He laid down His life for us. And we also ought to lay down our lives for the brethren. But whoever has this world's goods, and sees his brother in need, and shuts up his heart from him, how does the love of God abide in him? My little children, let us not love in word or in tongue, but in deed and in truth."*[347] Remember, Jesus said that we should lay up treasures in heaven and that we will be judged on how we have cared for others!

Acts tells about the hospitality of the early church.[348] People sold land and houses so that others would not be in need. Their generosity likely made it possible for new converts from far away to remain at Jerusalem and learn more of Jesus Christ. It also affected the community as multitudes of men and women responded to the gospel. We read of others in the churches of Asia sacrificing to send funds to Christians who lived where there was persecution or famine.[349]

Hospitality is still learned best by example. Perhaps you, too, have grandmothers who fed and housed visiting preachers or neighbors in need. Perhaps your parents have distributed needed food, clothes, and household goods. Perhaps families have opened their homes to you for fellowship, meals, or Bible study. Maybe you have been able to participate in works of service, missions, or other benevolence. If so, you have already learned that hospitality brings joy, and we are always blessed by those we seek to serve.

Do you hope to support your husband in ministry or as a deacon or elder in the Lord's church someday? Perhaps your spouse is serving now. A history of hospitality is a qualification for church leaders and their wives. Hospitality does not happen only at your residence. We should be welcoming to newcomers at church services and fellowship activities. We should make others feel welcome in the worship and work of the church. The wife of a minister, elder, or deacon does not have authority, but she certainly has the opportunity and responsibility to reach out to others and bring glory, not reproach, on the Lord's church.

There are great blessings for Christians who extend hospitality and give cheerfully. In doing so, we learn to trust God, glorify God, and love one another. Others are blessed, see the love of Christ in us, glorify God, and become open to the gospel to the saving of their souls. Read and make notes as you study this inspired passage from Paul to the church at Corinth.

2 CORINTHIANS 9:5-15

Therefore I thought it necessary to exhort the brethren to go to you ahead of time, and prepare your generous gift beforehand, which *you had* previously promised, that it may be ready as *a matter of* generosity and not as a grudging obligation.

> But this *I say:* He who sows sparingly will also reap sparingly, and he who sows bountifully will also reap bountifully. *So let* each one *give* as he purposes in his heart, not grudgingly or of necessity; for God loves a cheerful giver.
>
> And God *is* able to make all grace abound toward you, that you, always having all sufficiency in all *things,* may have an abundance for every good work. As it is written: *"He has dispersed abroad, He has given to the poor; His righteousness endures forever."*[350]
>
> Now may He who supplies seed to the sower, and bread for food, supply and multiply the seed you have *sown* and increase the fruits of your righteousness, while *you are* enriched in everything for all liberality, which causes thanksgiving through us to God.
>
> For the administration of this service not only supplies the needs of the saints, but also is abounding through many thanksgivings to God, while, through the proof of this ministry, they glorify God for the obedience of your confession to the gospel of Christ, and for *your* liberal sharing with them and all *men,* and by their prayer for you, who long for you because of the exceeding grace of God in you.
>
> Thanks *be* to God for His indescribable gift!

We will all stand at the throne of Christ and hear, *"Assuredly, I say to you, inasmuch as you did it to one of the least of these My brethren, you did it to Me."*[351] Since Jesus Christ gave His life for us, the Son of God died in the flesh to redeem created, sinful men and women, how can we claim to love one another or love Him and withhold our physical blessings when our neighbors are in need?[352] How can we not tell others of the gospel, the good news? Out of fervent love for one another, we will find great joy in opening our homes and sharing God's blessings with others![353]

SEVEN-POINT DISCUSSION GUIDE

1. False Teaching: Some people teach that giving to God assures material wealth. Many Scriptures address our giving, use of material possessions, and God's providence for His people. Choose one verse or passage and tell how it addresses part of this false doctrine.

2. What example did Barnabas set in Acts 4? What was the sin of Ananias and Sapphira?

3. How did Lydia feel about opening her home to the Apostle Paul and his fellow workers?

4. When we think of hospitality, what might we learn from Mary and Martha?

5. Why do we invite those to feasts who cannot return the favor?

6. How will our hospitality affect those to whom it is extended? How will it affect us?

7. What does Christ say about the care we extend to others in His name?

CALL TO ACTION
Set a goal for your growth in the work of the church through hospitality.

SONG AND PSALM

"SEEK YE FIRST" OR "GOD IS LOVE"

PSALM 112
Praise the Lord!

Blessed is the man who fears the Lord,
Who delights greatly in His commandments.

His descendants will be mighty on earth;
The generation of the upright will be blessed.
Wealth and riches will be in his house,
And his righteousness endures forever.

Unto the upright there arises light in the darkness;
He is gracious, and full of compassion, and righteous.

A good man deals graciously and lends;
He will guide his affairs with discretion.
Surely he will never be shaken;
The righteous will be in everlasting remembrance.

He will not be afraid of evil tidings;
His heart is steadfast, trusting in the Lord.
His heart is established;
He will not be afraid,
Until he sees his desire upon his enemies.

He has dispersed abroad,
He has given to the poor;
His righteousness endures forever;
His horn will be exalted with honor.

The wicked will see it and be grieved;
He will gnash his teeth and melt away;
The desire of the wicked shall perish.[354]

SUGGESTED TOPIC FOR PRAYER
Pray for eyes that see opportunities to care for others and for our daily bread!

UNIT 3

BE KEEPERS OF HIS CHURCH

"By this we know that we love the children of God, when we love God and keep His commandments. For this is the love of God, that we keep His commandments. And His commandments are not burdensome."

1 John 5:2-3

UNIT THREE INTRODUCTION

GOD'S DESIGN FOR HIS CHURCH

Lessons 8-10 teach about the roles we assume in Christ's church as followers, encouragers, and workers. The lessons will consider parallels between the unity of purpose of a honeybee colony and that of Christians in the church. This unit's lengthy introduction is meant to establish a base of understanding for the studies that follow.

God's amazing honeycomb has many functions, integral to every stage of life in a honeybee colony. Wax is secreted as flakes from glands in a bee's abdomen. Bees chew the flakes to soften them for use in honeycomb construction. Cells begin as staggered rows of cylinders, but the heat from the worker bees' bodies softens the wax, so neighboring cell walls merge to produce the strong, efficient, hexagonal shaped cells. Portions of the honeycomb have specific purposes; raising young, honey storage, and a dance floor where worker bees communicate the location of food sources with wiggles and turns. A honeybee colony cannot survive without a hive.

God's design for His church is far superior to the honeycomb. It is not a building that can be torn down, but His church is the people who wear the name of Jesus Christ. Together the church worships God, partakes of communion, sings, prays, does benevolent work, studies scripture, and evangelizes. We cannot have a relationship with Christ and not be a part of His church. Compare the practices of the Israelites under the Law of Moses (that ended with Christ's perfect sacrifice) and the practices of the church Christ redeemed with His blood.

God gave Moses detailed instructions for building the tabernacle in the wilderness and for the sacrifices people were to offer because of their sins. The tabernacle was a great tent built to God's exact specifications by the finest craftsmen available. It was carefully transported each time Israel moved from one location to another during their 40 years of wandering in the wilderness. God said the tabernacle represented things that are real in the heavens. When Solomon's temple was constructed in Jerusalem, it was carefully modeled after the design of the tabernacle, preserving the Holy Place and the Holy of Holies with the curtain that separated sinful man from the presence of God. When Christ died on the cross, the earth quaked, and the veil of separation was rent in two from the top to the bottom. In 70 AD, even Herod's rebuilding of the temple was destroyed along with genealogical records, rendering the practice of animal sacrifices under Mosaic Law impossible.

The church is not a physical building but is made of living stones — Christians. Christ is the cornerstone. In the New Testament, God gives exact instruction for the nature, mission, worship, organization, and service of His Church. During His ministry, Jesus taught His followers about the coming kingdom of God, His church, focusing almost exclusively on its nature and mission. This is recorded in the Gospels of Matthew, Mark, Luke, and John. God had planned His church before the foundation of the earth, but its mystery was not fully revealed until after Christ's death and resurrection. The Holy Spirit then guided its establishment through the work of the apostles and the writing of the New Testament. The church is ever under attack but will never succumb to the devil's onslaught. Indeed, death itself could not hold her Redeemer.[355]

If we do not understand that Jesus fulfilled and ended the Law of Moses recorded in the Old Testament, then we can become confused about God's plan for the church. Just as the tabernacle, sacrifices, and worship under the Mosaic Law had to meet God's exact specifications, only worship and adherence to God's plan in the New Testament will produce a church that is pleasing to Him. Here are critical differences in the Old Law, our schoolmaster, and the Words of Life delivered by Christ and the Apostles.

- The church of Christ is not a building made with hands. It is the people that God adds to His kingdom when they obey the gospel: repenting of sin, confessing Christ, being baptized into His death to wash away sin, and being raised from the water to walk in newness of life.
- Congregations may build a structure in which to meet, but it is like a beehive in a man-made apiary. We might call a wooden crate or woven basket a hive, but it's the work of God's bees that produces honeycomb and honey. Some call a building a church, but the church is the redeemed people of God. His church does not require a building.
- Christ's law is not written on stone tablets but on our hearts when we study and live according to the Bible, His inspired Truth. His Word enters our hearts when we listen to sound preaching, study God's Word, obey what it teaches, and pray for understanding and wisdom.
- Christians are not constrained to travel to one temple, city, or mountain to worship God. We do not have annual holy days set aside for worship. Instead, God seeks us to worship Him in spirit and in truth, willingly and purposefully, in every nation, on the first day of every week.
- We don't require priests to pray for us or offer animal sacrifices for our sins, for Christ was the perfect sacrifice that was offered once and for all. He is our High Priest. With the intercession of only the Holy Spirit, we can pray directly to God in Jesus' name. He who died for us also makes intercession for us before the Father. Therefore, those who have obeyed the gospel can boldly come before the throne of God. We are to call no man Father nor put a human in a role that detracts from the power of Jesus' sacrifice.
- We are not commanded to use trumpets or other musical instruments in Christian worship. In the New Testament we are commanded to sing hymns, psalms, and spiritual songs to praise God and edify one another.

- We are not required to keep feasts but humbly partake of the Lord's supper each Sunday to commemorate the sacrifice of the Lamb of God for our sins. We do so according to Christ's directions and the practices of the early church as recorded in the New Testament.
- We do not pay temple taxes and tithes. Christians are commanded to give freewill offerings as we have been prospered and as we purpose in our hearts. We also share what we have with those in need, never coveting another's belongings, never hoarding God's blessings, and never trusting in riches.
- We do not add to God's plan for His church, for it is perfect as He who designed it is perfect. Against God's will, the Israelites demanded an earthly king to be like the nations around them. Consequently, conceiving of themselves as an earthly kingdom became a barrier to their acceptance of Christ and His spiritual kingdom. Likewise, adding to God's plan for His church can prevent us from entering the kingdom.
- We call ourselves only by His name, for it was Christ who died to redeem us unto Himself. We strive to live sinless lives to glorify God and the name of Jesus Christ.
- We do not have a hierarchy of church officials and centralized church government under men. We have elders who care for each congregation according to God's commands, with only Christ as the head of the church. Christ is our King, because God gave Him all authority in heaven and earth after His resurrection. His will is in the Scriptures. The church is the kingdom of God on earth, which will be eternal in the heavens.[356]

The following three lessons address how we are to be followers, encouragers, and workers in the church.

LESSON 8

BE FOLLOWERS

"My sheep hear My voice, and I know them, and they follow Me."

—Jesus Christ, quoted in John 10:27

In this study, we will return to our three inseparable tenets of Christianity: Loving God, loving one another, and obeying God. Naturally, following Christ is the foundation for all of these. John compels us to be like Christ; loving one another as He loved us,[357] being purified as He is pure,[358] and walking as He walked.[359] Following Christ is a privilege extended to those who have ears to hear His voice[360] and willingness to surrender self.[361] As we follow Jesus, we abandon lives of sin to imitate Him, study the Bible to discern truth, and allow only Christ to rule His Kingdom, the church![362]

BEE-ATTITUDE: FOLLOW WILLINGLY

When food is abundant, a honeybee colony will grow until the hive is overcrowded. Overcrowding invites disease and mite infestation. Worker bees feed a special food secreted from glands on their heads to a few larvae. This royal jelly causes the larvae to mature into new queen bees instead of worker bees. Isn't that amazing?

A large swarm of bees will follow when a new queen takes flight. The swarm often lights in a tree, surrounds the queen bee, and sends scouts to search for a good hive location. When a suitable place is found, the swarm will follow the scouts to their new home.

Christians seek a new home with Jesus Christ because this world is marred by sin and death. We must follow Him, only Him. Though many antichrists have gone out into the world, none can destroy His church or assume His throne because all authority has been given to Him by God the Father.[363] We must follow Christ to secure eternal life in the kingdom. Jesus told His followers, *"I am the way, the truth, and the life. No one comes to the Father except through Me."* Jesus is our spiritual food,[364] our way,[365] and our king. Like a swarm of bees, we leave what is familiar to follow the One who has gone to prepare a place for us. Jesus promises, *"I will come again and receive you unto Myself; that where I am, there you may be also."*[366]

FOLLOW CHRIST

What does it mean to follow Christ? Jesus said, *"If anyone desires to come after Me, let him deny himself, and take up his cross and follow Me."*[367] Denying self means replacing our will with God's will. Though Jesus is the eternal Son of God, He emptied Himself and came to earth as the Son of Man, saying, *"For I have come down from heaven, not to do My own will, but the will of Him who sent Me."*[368] There was no need for Jesus to do differently.[369] He came to do the will of His Father. He wanted to bring glory to God's name.

The same is true for you and me. A Christian woman can confidently conform her will to God's will, because God's law is perfect.[370] As we put our faith into action, we find joy. When we choose not to sin, we avoid its negative consequences. We invest our time and talents in good works, and that pleases the Lord.[371] We care for our families and love our husbands as the Lord commands, and our homes are blessed.[372] We do our jobs as unto the Lord, not as men- pleasers, and our work is blessed.[373]

Setting aside worldly things makes room for a more abundant life in Christ.[374] As we experience the abundance of Christian living, we find our will becomes more like God's will for us.

Jesus provided a miraculous catch of fish on the morning before he called Peter, James, and John to leave their nets and follow Him. The men had fished the Sea of Galilee all night and caught nothing, but at Jesus' word, they let their nets down again. So many fish filled their nets that the nets began to break.[375] Overcome by the power and holiness of Jesus, Peter fell at His feet and begged, *"Depart from me, for I am a sinful man, O Lord!"*[376]

Jesus did not offer His disciples a six-figure salary and a 401K to follow Him but much, much more! *"Then He said to them, 'Follow Me, and I will make you fishers of men.'"*[377] The disciples' purpose in life changed. Their pursuits became spiritual. Their catch became eternal souls! Today, 21 centuries after their departure from this earth, the apostles' example and epistles continue to convert our souls. God continues to provide the increase!*[378]

One of the richest Bible studies for the new or mature Christian is the life of Christ in the Gospels. All Scripture comes from the mind of God, but those red-lettered books show us how God completed His plan to redeem man through the life, death, and resurrection of Jesus.[379] They reveal the message of Christ, *"Believe and repent!"*[380] In the Gospels, our belief is born and nurtured by the fulfillment of centuries of prophecy. Our faith that Jesus is the Christ is affirmed by the testimony of God's voice from heaven. It is compelled by Jesus' miracles and resurrection, the words and lives of the apostles, and eyewitnesses accounts of His miraculous works. In the Gospels of Matthew, Mark, Luke, and John, we can see Jesus address the sins of people just like us. We hear His sermons. We see the Son of God humbly live as the Son of Man and die for our redemption. Finally, in the Gospels, we learn of His resurrection and invitation to all nations to be baptized in the name of the Father, Son, and Holy Spirit and observe all things He has commanded! The gospels preach what it means to follow Christ.

Jesus taught us to fulfill the two great commandments of loving God with all our heart, soul, and mind and loving our neighbor as ourselves.[381] Sin is the opposite. Though the world seeks to rename and justify sin, it is always against God and almost always against others.

Consider stealing, lies, fornication, and adultery. Consider idolatry, taking God's name in vain, false teaching, and coveting what belongs to others. Consider murder, failing to spread the gospel, and refusing to care for our family, parents, or others in need. List these or other sins in your own words, and write how they violate the great commandments:

MATTHEW 22:37-40, QUOTING DEUTERONOMY 6:5

"Jesus said to him, '"You shall love the Lord your God with all your heart, with all your soul, and with all your mind.' This is the first and great commandment.

And *the* second *is* like it: 'You shall love your neighbor as yourself.'

On these two commandments hang all the Law and the Prophets."[382]

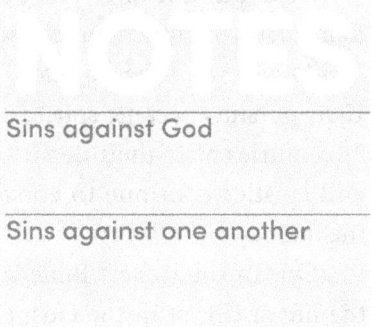

Sins against God

Sins against one another

WALK AS HE WALKED

A precious hymn of encouragement is William Ogden's "Where He Leads Me, I Will Follow." It says of Christ, "He the great example is, and pattern for me." John says we must walk as Jesus walked. This walk is the way we live our lives. Jesus did not walk among the Jewish elite, earthly governors, or kings.[383] He did not enter a city with trumpets or gather mighty men to do His bidding.[384] He went where people needed Him. He went to those who were open to God's message.[385] He went preaching the gospel and healing the sick.[386] He did not draw back from sinners, publicans, Pharisees, Samaritans, Romans, Gentiles, or even lepers.[387] He did not charge for His sermons. He did not alter the truth to please men.[388] He sought God's guidance in prayer and allowed His Father to direct His steps.[389]

Jesus walked humbly.[390] He did not come to earth to be glorified and served by man. He lived among common people, owned no house, and assumed no office. He went where the Spirit sent Him and where God, His Father, bid Him go…even to the cross. On the cross, He prayed that God would forgive those who put Him there. We all have sinned and share in the guilt of those who drove the nails into His hands and feet.

Jesus' humility, love, and grace are most beautifully demonstrated by the way He dealt with Peter's denial. He prayed for Simon Peter, knowing he would deny Him. He warned Peter that he would deny Him three times before the rooster crowed. Amid Jesus' trial proceedings, He was still mindful of Peter being in spiritual danger and looked at him. In remorse, Peter wept bitterly.

After His death and resurrection, Jesus met Peter's boat at the water's edge where He had first called Peter to follow Him. Again, Jesus directed the Apostles where to cast their nets for an overwhelming catch of fish. When John recognized Christ, Peter jumped into the sea to swim ashore. Jesus was waiting by a fire of coals. There He asked Peter to reaffirm His love for Him and restored Peter to the work he was called to do![391]

We must walk humbly to follow Christ.[392] We cannot befriend this world and imagine ourselves to be the friend of Jesus.[393] We cannot draw back from our brother and say we love God.[394] We must walk in the light.[395] Christ said, *"Walk while you have the light, lest darkness overtake you; he who walks in darkness does not know where he is going."*[396] Walking in the light involves doing the work God has for us to do, "For we are His workmanship, created in Christ Jesus for good works, which God prepared beforehand that we should walk in them."[397]

Will we sin? Yes, but faithful Christians do not choose to continue in it. Must we repent and avoid sin? Yes. Can we cease to walk in Christ? Yes, we can lose our salvation if we return to walking after the flesh.[398] John identifies those who have fallen away, saying, *"Whoever does not practice righteousness is not of God, nor is he who does not love his brother."*[399] The source of a Christian's great peace is declared in 1 John 1:7, *"But if we walk in the light as He is in the light, we have fellowship with one another, and the blood of Jesus Christ His Son cleanses us from all sin."*[400] Can we be restored if we fall away? Yes, just as Christ restored Peter, He will accept us if we repent of sin and return to do as He commands us.[401] Is there a grave danger of being lost if a Christian returns to sin? Yes. The danger is that our hearts will harden beyond repentance if we desire sin enough to disregard the sacrifice of Christ.[402]

Note the connections made among obedience, repentance, the Word of God, and the love of God in 1 John 2:1-6.

1 JOHN 2:1-6

"My little children, these things I write to you, so that you may not sin. And **if anyone sins, we have an Advocate with the Father, Jesus Christ the righteous.**

And **He Himself is the propitiation for our sins**, and not for ours only but also for the whole world.

Now by this we know that we know Him, if we **keep His commandments.**

He who says, "I know Him," and does not **keep His commandments**, is a liar, and the **truth** is not in him.

But whoever **keeps His word**, truly **the love of God** is perfected in him. By this we know that we are in Him.

He who says he abides in Him ought himself also to **walk just as He walked.**"

LOVE ONE ANOTHER AS JESUS LOVES

Jesus took the commandment to love one another and made it new, adding that we are to love one another <u>as He loves us; He gave Himself for us</u>.[403] Would you give your life for your husband, parent, child, or dearest friend? Would you die to protect a brother or sister in Christ? Would you die for someone who was always in opposition to you, always doing what you asked him or her not to do? Jesus did. I was one of those rebellious sinners who necessitated His sacrifice. You were, too. If Jesus loves us that way, forgives our sins though our sins put Him on the cross, how ought we to act toward others He died to save?

When you feel yourself hesitating to interact with another person, look for the work of the devil in the moment. James says that when we show partiality toward people, we have *"become judges with evil thoughts."*[404] Instead, we ought to think, *Our Lord died for her, will you and I share our physical blessings with her? Our Lord died for him, will you and I risk embarrassment to tell him so? Is she worthy of our time? Will we forgive those who offend us, even if they do not apologize or make restitution for wrongs they have done? Will we make friends of God's children when they look, act, speak, or dress differently? 'When they must fight sin that is controlling their lives? Will we teach the truth in love to those who oppose us?*

We have been called to be a peculiar people, set apart for God's purposes.[405] It is the greatest calling ever extended to a person. It offers the greatest reward a human can aspire to attain! As societies become increasingly given to sin, like Cain toward Abel, people will be offended because our works are good when theirs are evil.[406] Sometimes Jesus' words may seem harsh, but He came to save the lost. To repent of sin, we must first be convicted in our hearts of sin. We must realize our eternal fate is at stake!

Noah's flood delivered the righteous patriarch from a sinful generation as the waters of baptism now save us. How many people discourage baptism today![407] Unbelievers also endangered the man who hesitated to follow Christ in Matthew 8, so our Lord said, *"Follow Me, and let the dead bury their own dead."*[408] Though we are to love all others, we are not to be dissuaded by, participate in, condone, or encourage evil works.[409] When anything in this world is a barrier to following Christ, we must sever it from our lives. Christ made this point with the poignant imagery of cutting off a hand or foot that offends. He reminds us that the reward we seek is eternal life. The consequences for failure are the undying flames of hell, far worse than even maiming the physical body.[410]

With heaven and hell in mind, consider, do material possessions and money threaten to bar you from following Him? Jesus said, *"If you want to be perfect, go, sell what you have and give to the poor, and you will have treasure in heaven; and come, follow Me."*[411] Does the cost of discipleship in human relationships seem great to you? Christ knew it would, but promised, *"Assuredly, I say to you, there is no one who has left house or parents or brothers or wife or children, for the sake of the kingdom of God, who shall not receive many times more in this present time, and in the age to come eternal life."*[412] Does persecution frighten you? We are not to even love our lives, for Jesus said, *"Whoever desires to come after Me, let him deny himself, and* take up his cross, and follow Me."[413] And, *"Whosoever shall seek to save his life shall lose it; and whosoever shall lose his life shall preserve it."*[414]

Now, return to the commandment to love one another as Christ loves us. Peter wrote about having compassion for one another in 1 Peter 3:8-17, quoting promises from Psalm 34:12-16 that God sees and hears the prayers of those who do good. Paul wrote to the church at Corinth that all sacrifices are nothing unless done out of love.[415] Read and reflect on this description of charity, love in action. Make notes about how this love manifests in your Christian walk.

1 CORINTHIANS 13:4–7

> Love suffers long *and* is kind;
> love does not envy;
> love does not parade itself,
> is not puffed up;
> does not behave rudely,
> does not seek its own,
> is not provoked,
> thinks no evil;
> does not rejoice in iniquity,
> but rejoices in the truth;
> bears all things,
> believes all things,
> hopes all things,
> endures all things.[416]

DISCERN THE TRUTH

If we are to follow Christ, we must know His teachings.[417] We must be able to distinguish truth from lies, false teaching, and doctrines of this world. First Peter 3:13 reads, *"And who is he who will harm you if you become followers of what is good?"* Peter wrote that even if we are persecuted for our faith, it is a blessing. Love the truth! Think of the powerful and urgent cry of a tiny infant who is hungry. That is how we are to *"desire the pure milk of the word, that you may grow thereby."*[418]

Be confident that God's Word is truth.[419] The more time you spend studying Scripture, the more your heart will be secured.[420] The Bible is the

Word of God, the Word of Life.[421] In the gospel, the righteousness of God is revealed.[422] Through obedience to the Word, we can be born again.[423] If the Word of God abides in us, we can overcome the wicked one.[424]

Non-believers and false teachers serve the devil as they casually toss criticism at the Bible. They convince themselves and the unlearned person to discount the only source of truth. Many people are gullible and willingly doubt the power of God's Word without ever investigating The Holy Book. Many do not want to be held responsible to God, so they avoid religion. Some scientists and others become smug in knowledge and challenge the existence of God and things they cannot yet see. How recently were we ignorant of atoms? Of DNA? Of nano particles? Consider the supremacy of our Creator. Kyle Butts (2023) wrote that a spoonful of DNA could hold all the knowledge, visual imagery, art, and writings of mankind. How foolish to discount God and His Word, the Bible, the handbook He provided for living life, the record of man's origins and purpose!

Peter wrote, *"For we did not follow cunningly devised fables when we made known to you the power and coming of our Lord Jesus Christ, but were eyewitnesses of His majesty."*[425] No book has ever been so carefully examined, as continually before the eyes of man and scholar, or so often verified by external sources, scientific discoveries, and archaeological evidence. Yet all the verification needed is between its pages, for Scripture allows man to see into the perfect mind of God.[426]

The Word of God defends against false prophets who blaspheme Christianity and draw many into condemnation. Knowing the Scriptures is our defense against false teachers.

Deceivers prey upon those who are caught up in sin and lust, those Paul called gullible women who were always learning but never able to arrive at truth.[427] What makes a person gullible? If we try to hold on to this world, we will not have ears to hear the truth. We cannot hijack grace and continue in the sins we choose.[428] When women or men accept something other than God's Word, they are not saved, they are not serving God, and they are not good enough people that they can make their own entrance into heaven. Those who bring false teaching are not progressive and insightful but hypocritical and wicked. Those who follow them are lost.[429]

What is the gospel? The glad tidings angels brought to the shepherds in Bethlehem's pastures were that Jesus Christ was born. Noel! Jesus came in the flesh to live a sinless life and teach repentance to Israel. By the will of God, He died as a perfect sacrifice for the sins of all mankind and was resurrected the third day in victory over sin and death! Thus, baptized into His death, our sins can be removed, and we, too, can rise to walk as He walked. Jesus ascended into heaven, and His church was established a few days later, on the Day of Pentecost. Those who believe, repent, and are baptized are added to His church by God. If we live obediently unto death, we will inherit eternal life. Those who do not believe and obey the gospel will be lost, condemned to hell eternally. *Gospel* means "good news" because without Christ's death and resurrection, all the animal sacrifices of mankind would have had no effect. All of creation would have been condemned to death and eternal separation from the Creator, for all have sinned.

False teachers all change the gospel in some way. They put men or women in place of Christ. They suggest that grace excludes obedience or that works negate grace. They deny that Christ came in the flesh, or they say there are many other sons of God. They question the accuracy of God's Word or rewrite it to accommodate their lies. They accept man's doctrines and replace God's Word with man's words. They question God's precepts: creation, truth, love, sin, family, redemption, justice, mercy, worship, right, wrong, gender roles, gender, heaven, and hell. They offer many 'churches.' They teach that men and women can choose how to worship and be saved. They blame God for human suffering. They deny His creation, His existence, and His power. None of this affects the nature of God or changes truth.[430] The problem is that the devil destroys souls with these lies.

Paul wrote to Christians who were being misled by false teachers, *"I marvel that you are turning away so soon from Him who called you in the grace of Christ, to a different gospel, which is not another; but there are some who trouble you and want to pervert the gospel of Christ. But even if we, or an angel from heaven, preach any other gospel to you than what we have preached to you, let him be accursed. As we have said before, so now I say again, if anyone preaches any other gospel to you than what you have received, let him be accursed. For do I now persuade men, or God? Or do*

I seek to please men? For if I still pleased men, I would not be a bondservant of Christ."[431]

ALLOW ONLY CHRIST TO LEAD HIS CHURCH

When we imitate a fellow Christian, it is insofar as that person is following God's Word. This means we must each know how to distinguish sound doctrine from false teaching.[432] Paul invited others to follow his example because he followed Jesus Christ. Led by the Holy Spirit, Paul made sure to establish the authority of Christ over every man, including himself. *"Imitate me, just as I also imitate Christ.*[433] *Now I praise you, brethren, that you remember me in all things and keep the traditions just as I delivered them to you. But I want you to know that the head of every man is Christ, the head of woman is man, and the head of Christ is God."*[434] Every father, husband, preacher, elder, man, and woman is subject to Christ — as were the apostles.[435]

Paul compares his subjection to Christ's authority to the relationship of a woman to her husband. Some may wince at this, but why? Paul also compares that subjection to the subjection of Christ to God, the Father. This submission of wills is about a trusting relationship in which the leader is always subject to the authority of our Holy, Merciful, Faithful Creator. When a preacher, teacher, friend, or spouse departs from God's will, we must follow our Lord. God -> Christ -> Man -> Wife: Dear sisters in Christ, glorify God by doing His will in all things. Teach your daughters that living in subjection to Christ and to their husbands is a high calling that takes dedication and faith. Teach your sons that they must lead their homes, fully subjecting themselves to Christ, loving their wives as Christ loves the church and died for it.

A godly preacher is the means by which God chose to spread the gospel.[436] Those who preach and teach must carefully communicate God's Word and His will. As Christians, we may be edified in our walk by the example of faithful brothers and sisters. Yet, one must be an imitator of Christ to be a suitable model. Those who teach are subjected to greater scrutiny at judgment.[437] We are warned that it is a grievous sin to cause the loss of one for whom Christ died.[438] Most of us are both followers and leaders. Mature women are to teach younger women. We are to teach the children. Our words and conduct influence our friends and families. Even our songs edify one another. What a challenge is accepted when we sing such words as these from Charles Wesley's stirring hymn!

A charge to keep I have,
A God to glorify,
A never-dying soul to save,
And fit it for the sky.

To serve the present age,
My calling to fulfill;
Oh, may it all my pow'rs engage
To do my Master's will!

FOLLOWERSHIP

The world sees a paradox when it looks at Christianity. Our leaders are servants. The person who serves others is the greatest in the kingdom. Our King not only humbled Himself to wash the feet of His disciples but was willing to sacrifice Himself on the cross to redeem us from our sins! Out of the purest love, the sinless Son of God died to redeem His fallen creation, sinful mankind. Jesus did so to fulfill God's plan, to do His Father's will. We are most certainly commanded to do the same.

Jesus Christ humbled Himself to be obedient to God, to glorify God, and to complete the work God sent Him to do. God praised Jesus from the heavens for His obedience and sat Him at His right hand upon His ascension. Read and make notes on this passage:

PHILIPPIANS 2:5-11

Let this mind be in you which was also in Christ Jesus, who, being in the form of God, did not consider it robbery to be equal with God,

but made Himself of no reputation, taking the form of a bondservant, *and* coming in the likeness of men.

> And being found in appearance as a man,
> He humbled Himself and became obedient to *the point of* death, even the death of the cross.
>
> Therefore God also has highly exalted Him and given Him the name which is above every name, that at the name of Jesus every knee should bow, of those in heaven, and of those on earth, and of those under the earth,
>
> and *that* every tongue should confess that Jesus Christ *is* Lord, to the glory of God the Father.[439]

Informed by Jesus' obedient sacrifice, women are not belittled by subjection to their husbands or by assuming only the roles God has assigned us in the church and family. When we live as God instructs in a Christian home or in His church, we are elevated to be an example to the world, to be part of things that transcends this life as nothing else does or can.

Men are not demeaned to do just what the Bible commands. We surrender human innovations and doctrines to His glory! The church is Christ's. Only He died for it. Christians are only approved by God when we do His will. Indeed, we will be welcomed into heaven only if we have cared for one another and obeyed His commandments.

BIBLICAL EXAMPLES OF NOT FOLLOWING GOD

People have long speculated about where Cain got his wife, but the Scriptures clearly say Eve was the mother of all living.[440] This misconception arises from reading the only inspired account of the first family as if Abel, Cain, and Seth were Adam and Eve's only offspring. Genesis 4:3-4 says Adam lived 930 years and had sons and daughters. There are many things we wonder about the people and events concisely recorded in the Bible, but we are not to get distracted by useless disputes or men's fables. All Scripture is there for God's purposes, carefully preserved by the Holy Spirit to reveal truth and instruct us in righteousness. The tragic conflict between Cain and Abel informs all of mankind. Abel's death affected the lineage of Christ. His murder at the hands of Cain shows the insidious nature of envy and how hatred in a person's heart leads to sin and death.[441]

Their story demonstrates the importance of being a follower of God's will and the terrible consequences of putting our desires ahead of His commands. The brothers' conflict began when Abel followed God's will in worship by offering the firstborn of his flock to God while Cain chose to bring an offering of the grain he had raised as a farmer. God's exact commands to Cain and Abel for worship are not recorded but knowing them is not necessary for us to gain understanding. They were to do God's will. With our knowledge of Scripture, we can see that Abel's sacrifice foreshadowed God's sacrifice of Jesus Christ. God warned Cain that his jealousy would lead to sin and that he needed to get himself under control.[442] Rather than heed God's warning and repent, Cain took his brother's life. As part of his punishment, God said that when he tilled the ground, it would no longer yield its strength to Cain.

Aaron, the brother of Moses and High Priest, had two sons who served before the Lord. They had even been allowed to come into the presence of God. God gave Aaron specific directions for His worship. In Leviticus 10 we are told that Nadab and Abihu came before the Lord with censers with fire in them and incense on them unlike what God had commanded.[443] *"So fire went out from the Lord and devoured them, and they* died before the Lord. And Moses said to Aaron, "This is what the Lord spoke, saying: 'By those who come near Me I must be regarded as holy; And before all the people I must be *glorified.*'"[444] God did not even allow their father and brothers to mourn Nadab and Abihu but had them buried outside the camp. We are not told why Cain, Nadab, or Abihu chose to alter God's commands. Man's motives for disobedience do not matter because it is not man's prerogative to alter God's will. It is covetous, blasphemous, and evil to desire to take what is God's.

The same envy among the Jewish religious leaders motivated the crucifixion of Jesus Christ. They wanted to preserve their power even if it meant falsely accusing and executing the Son of God.[445] After Christ ascended and the church was established, Rome destroyed Jerusalem and the temple in A.D. 70 as Christ foretold. God brought an end to the Jews' rebellious religious leadership. God does not yield the rule of His people to men or demons. Neither do men nor women have the right to change God's will for the nature, work, or worship of the church.

APPLICATION IN OUR LIVES

Today, over 30,000 denominations call themselves Christian, but Christ died for His church. Many denominations have been created to suit human ideas and satisfy things that people want from a church by human innovation. Yet, God has clearly specified what He seeks from those who worship Him. Jesus said we must worship Him in spirit and in truth. Paul tells us there is one church.[446] Luke tells us in Acts that God adds those who are saved to His church.[447] There will be no divine separation of the false teachers and their followers from the faithful until the end of this age.[448] We are all given responsibility to study Scriptures to discern the truth from lies and the righteous from the wicked.[449] If humans choose to do their will instead of God's will, the separation will come at the judgment. Christ will know His own, and those who do not know God will depart into everlasting condemnation.[450]

Following Christ as He wills, as God the Father wills, is the commitment we make as Christians. Faith includes belief, trust, and obedience. As we mature in Christ and experience His providence, we find it easier to relinquish what we once perceived as control of our lives. Scripture says if we do not serve God, we serve evil. Sometimes our self-direction is sin that we allow to remain in our lives. We fight a spiritual battle but are also carnal beings.[451] The battle we fight against evil is not fought alone, for God is our Commander and King. Christians rely on God who knows all and has all power to direct our way.[452] His way is far above our understanding, but because He loves us and Christ died to redeem us, we can place all trust in Him.[453] His will is perfect. He can keep the souls that are committed to Him. Following Christ brings unmatched joy and gladness even in this world.

- The lives we lead here are more abundant when we serve Christ.
- Our relationships with others are based on love and responsibility.
- Living your life forgiven of sin is true freedom.

- Lives guided by righteousness bring God's peace and joy.[454]
- Encouragement, edification toward good works, and support during times of hardship characterize our relationships with our brothers and sisters in Christ.
- Prayer, Bible study, and worship allow us to communicate with our loving Creator.
- The most precious blessing of our faith is being restored to fellowship with God the Father, Jesus Christ, and the Holy Spirit.
- Even when faith brings persecution, we are promised a reward that is so great we can leap for joy![455]

SEVEN-POINT DISCUSSION GUIDE

1. False Teaching: Some people teach that we can follow the doctrines of men and obtain salvation if our hearts are sincere. Why is this an error according to Scripture?

2. The prophet Ezekiel lived during the second wave of Babylonian captivity. He wrote, "The word of the LORD came again to me, saying: *'Son of man, when a land sins against Me by persistent unfaithfulness, I will stretch out My hand against it; I will cut off its supply of bread, send famine on it, and cut off man and beast from it. Even if these three men, Noah, Daniel, and Job, were in it, they would deliver only themselves by their righteousness,'* says the Lord God."[456] What do we know about the lives of Noah, Daniel, and Job?

3. Following requires trust in your leader. What traits do you look for in a human leader? Why is trust well-placed in the Lord as our Leader?

4. Why does it elevate a woman to submit to the leadership of her husband and assume only the roles God has assigned to her in His church?

5. People justify "innovations" in worship as "ways to accomplish what God has commanded." How can we know whether we are violating God's will for worship?

6. God has not accepted changes men make to His commands for worship since the beginning of time. We studied the acts of Cain, Nadab and Abihu, and the Jewish leaders who had Jesus executed. Can you think of another biblical example of people supplanting God's will in worship? What was the outcome?

7. Who died for the church? Who should lead the church? Who should direct our individual lives? Who is seated on the right hand of God? Who will judge us in the last day?

CALL TO ACTION

- Pray for help in learning to submit to God's will. Pray specific prayers when faced with big decisions or if you are struggling to do as He asks.
- Choose one or two Scriptures that address submitting to God's will that can strengthen you, and put them by your door or in other places where you will read them daily.
- Keep a diary about your submission to God's will: Note times you alter or make decisions after considering God's will. Note times you put your will before God's will. Note what happens when you do God's will. Note God's answers to your prayers.

SONG OR PSALM

"WHERE HE LEADS ME, I WILL FOLLOW"
"THE PROVIDENCE OF GOD"

SUGGESTED TOPIC FOR PRAYER
Pray for help in learning to submit to God's will.

LESSON 9

BE ENCOURAGERS

"Therefore let us pursue the things which make for peace and the things by which one may edify another."

Romans 14:19

Jesus did not ask of us to wear peculiar clothing or ornaments to demark us as His followers. Instead, He commanded us to have such a relationship with others that everyone would recognize us as His disciples. *"A new commandment I give to you, that you love one another; as I have loved you, that you also love one another. By this all will know that you are My disciples, if you have love for one another."*[457] Thus Christians pursue peace with one another and seek to edify, to build-up one another, in the most Holy Faith.

BEE-ATTITUDE: ENCOURAGING

Honey and the honeycomb are known to encourage healing. Recent, renewed interest in holistic wound care has resulted in adhesive bandages infused with honey being available at most pharmacies. Honey's antioxidants help reduce inflammation. Its antibiotic properties reduce the chance of infection. Wax from the honeycomb can seal out impurities and preserve skin's moisture to promote healing.

Similarly, Christians are to encourage one another's spiritual well-being. Worshiping God with other Christians is commanded on the first day of every week. Assembling to worship is His will and the primary occasion for the saints to edify one another!

ENCOURAGEMENT IN THE CHURCH

Jesus desires His church to portray the love He has for us, the love that motivated Him to be sacrificed to redeem our souls, the love that forgives our sins and motivates our risen Savior to bring us to be with Him eternally. The Lord's Supper is a weekly remembrance of Jesus' sacrifice that calls us to repentance. It is also called communion because we partake of it together, the assembled church in fellowship with our Redeemer. Prayers and Scriptures shared while partaking of the bread and fruit-of-the-vine often encourage all to be penitent and grateful for our salvation in Christ. Congregational prayer and praise deepen our faith in God. Studying the Bible and sound preaching encourage our spiritual growth. We are to sing with understanding because God planned for song to be a way we edify one another.

When one is baptized into Christ, the tears of joy and warm welcome of brothers and sisters reflect the rejoicing in heaven when a sinner comes to repentance. When an erring Christian responds to the gospel invitation to ask for prayers for restoration in Christ, the welcoming forgiveness of the church is reassuring. Christian fellowship makes it easier to avoid sin. Doing the work of the church together helps us mature in Christ. Elders who know each member well can recognize and address sin that threatens our spiritual health. During times of trials, we can seek guidance from more mature sisters or brothers. When we undertake a new work or suffer illness, the church may provide support and pray on our behalf. How precious is the edification that comes from Christian fellowship!

Examine these Scriptures, and note the role of edification in each function of worship:

SCRIPTURES RELATED TO CORPORATE WORSHIP

Assembly
"And let us consider one another in order to stir up love and good works, not forsaking the assembling of ourselves together, as *is* the manner of some, but exhorting *one another,* and so much the more as you see the Day approaching."[458]

The Lord's Supper/Communion
"The cup of blessing which we bless, is it not the communion of the blood of Christ? The bread which we break, is it not the communion of the body of Christ? For we, *though* many, are one bread *and* one body; for we all partake of that one bread."[459]

Prayer and Repentance
"Confess *your* trespasses to one another, and pray for one another, that you may be healed. The effective, fervent prayer of a righteous man avails much."[460]

Preaching
— *From Paul, Silvanus, and Timothy to church at Thessalonica* "You *are* witnesses, and God *also,* how devoutly and justly and blamelessly we behaved ourselves among you who believe; as you know how we exhorted, and comforted, and charged every one of you, as a father *does* his own children, that you would walk worthy of God who calls you into His own kingdom and glory."[461]

Teaching
"And He Himself gave some *to be* apostles, some prophets, some evangelists, and some pastors and teachers, for the equipping of the saints for the work of ministry, for the edifying of the body of Christ,"[462]

Singing
"Let the word of Christ dwell in you richly in all wisdom, teaching and admonishing one another in psalms and hymns and spiritual songs, singing with grace in your hearts to the Lord."[463]

Giving
"On the first *day* of the week let each one of you lay something aside, storing up as he may prosper, that there be no collections when I come."[464]

Obedience to the Gospel
"Only let your conduct be worthy of the gospel of Christ, so that whether I come and see you or am absent, I may hear of your affairs, that you stand fast in one spirit, with one mind striving together for the faith of the gospel, and not in any way terrified by your adversaries, which is to them a proof of perdition, but to you of salvation, and that from God."[465]

ENCOURAGEMENT AND EDIFICATION

The goals of edification are saving souls and maintaining the purity of the church. The New Testament books of Romans; 1 & 2 Corinthians; Galatians; Ephesians; Philippians; Colossians; 1 & 2 Thessalonians; Hebrews; James; 1 & 2 Peter; 1, 2, & 3 John, and Jude were written by Paul and other Apostles to the churches. The books of 1 & 2 Timothy, Titus, and Philemon were written by Paul to individuals. Before they were gathered into New Testament form, they were hand-copied and passed among congregations. Imagine how eagerly they were received! The letters encourage preachers, congregations, and their elderships.

Each epistle is filled with edification from the inspired writer and commands for all Christians to admonish or edify one another; *"Therefore comfort each other and edify one another, just as you also are doing,"*[466] and *"Therefore let us pursue the things which make for peace and the things by which one may edify another."*[467]

Edification can be words of encouragement, teaching, songs and psalms, prayers, donations to Christian ministries, listening, counseling, discouraging sin, fellowship, or removing barriers so others may study God's Word or work on benevolent projects. Growing in the faith is different from the pursuit of worldly achievements. We are to seek the best for others rather than compete with one another! Our edification is to be in God, toward obedience, and motivated by our love for one another.

To grow in the work of edification, study the encouraging words of the apostles to the churches. *"Since you have purified your souls in obeying the truth through the Spirit in sincere love of the brethren, love one another fervently with a pure heart."*[468] Then, examine yourself. Are you purifying your soul by obeying the truth? Do you have a sincere love of the brethren? Do you love others with a pure heart? Examine your prayers. Are you asking God to do your will or are you asking to know His will so that you can do it?

Do you need encouragement? Do not hesitate to seek it from God in prayer and through fellowship with others in Christ. Turn to the Bible. Inspired and preserved by the providence of the Holy Spirit, the apostles' messages of admonishment remain to edify every generation as the New Testament. While there are many blessings in Christian fellowship, we are not to focus on whether others are doing things for us, but on how we can be of service to others and please God. The cure for discouragement is to remember the faith of those who came before and the sacrifice of Christ Jesus.[469]

Consider one of Paul's messages of edification. Note the attitudes and actions he encouraged.

COLOSSIANS 3:12-16

"Therefore, as *the* elect of God, holy and beloved,

put on tender mercies, kindness, humility, meekness, longsuffering;

bearing with one another, and forgiving one another,

> if anyone has a complaint against another; even as Christ forgave you, so you also *must do*.
>
> But above all these things put on love, which is the bond of perfection.
>
> And let the peace of God rule in your hearts, to which also you were called in one body; and be thankful.
>
> Let the word of Christ dwell in you richly in all wisdom, teaching and admonishing one another in psalms and hymns and spiritual songs, singing with grace in your hearts to the Lord."[470]

We all need edification. We imitate our Lord when we offer it to others. How precious are God's words of encouragement to Jesus after His obedience in baptism! *"It came to pass in those days that Jesus came from Nazareth of Galilee, and was baptized by John in the Jordan. And immediately, coming up from the water, He saw the heavens parting and the Spirit descending upon Him like a dove. Then a voice came from heaven,* **"You are My beloved Son, in whom I am well pleased."**[471]

ENCOURAGEMENT IN TIMES OF NEED

Some of the happiest times in our lives can be times of vulnerability. Newlyweds, new parents, new jobs in new towns with increased responsibility, and going away to college are occasions when Christians are tempted to neglect attendance to worship or entertain ideas that go against the Truth. It is invaluable to have Christian sisters and brothers who look for you at services, offer to help with young children, invite you into their homes, and ask you to be part of the work of the church. Older Christians who have experienced the challenges you are now facing can offer encouragement to put the things of God first. Prayers and godly examples of others in your same stage of life can be edifying, showing you ways to manage your responsibilities and the blessings that come from faithfulness. Seeing others overcome greater trials can strengthen us to endure and rely on God.

Be Encouragers

When we are elderly, critically ill, disabled, or know that we are dying, we have an opportunity to encourage others who may face the same trials a little later. My daughter went away to a state university, hours from home. She attended a large congregation there. The college Bible class was taught by a precious brother, Todd Walker, who had just been diagnosed with ALS. His courage and God's strength led him to continue teaching that class for many months as the awful disease weakened his body. His wife, son, and daughter were often in the class as well, providing help and testifying with their faithfulness. He spoke openly of his choice to refuse experimental therapies that used fetal tissue from aborted babies. His lessons focused on the grace of Christ and trusting in His forgiveness. Todd's testimony strengthened my daughter and many others against the godless indoctrination that often characterizes university educations. It can be tempting to focus on what we cannot do and succumb to frustration, but God can certainly use us in our hours of hardship. Paul wrote, "Therefore I take pleasure in infirmities, in reproaches, in needs, in persecutions, in distresses, for Christ's sake. For when I am weak, then I am strong."[472]

Encouragement can be drawn from the faith of others. Those who faithfully endure persecution become a beacon of hope and an example of trust in Christ that prepares us to persevere. Read and take notes on this passage from Paul to the church at Thessalonica when he was imprisoned as the Holy Spirit foretold. What is the effect of communication between this church and Paul? It is similar to when we support neighboring congregations, missionaries, and members when they are away from home.

ENCOURAGEMENT FROM PAUL WHEN THE THESSALONIANS FACED PERSECUTION

1 THESSALONIANS 3:1-13

"Therefore, when we could no longer endure it, we thought it good to be left in Athens alone, and sent Timothy, our brother and minister of God, and our fellow laborer in the gospel of Christ, to establish you and encourage you concerning your faith, that

no one should be shaken by these afflictions; for you yourselves know that we are appointed to this.

For, in fact, we told you before when we were with you that we would suffer tribulation, just as it happened, and you know. For this reason, when I could no longer endure it, I sent to know your faith, lest by some means the tempter had tempted you, and our labor might be in vain.

But now that Timothy has come to us from you, and brought us good news of your faith and love, and that you always have good remembrance of us, greatly desiring to see us, as we also *to see* you — therefore, brethren, in all our affliction and distress we were comforted concerning you by your faith. For now we live, if you stand fast in the Lord.

For what thanks can we render to God for you, for all the joy with which we rejoice for your sake before our God, night and day praying exceedingly that we may see your face and perfect what is lacking in your faith?

Now may our God and Father Himself, and our Lord Jesus Christ, direct our way to you. And may the Lord make you increase and abound in love to one another and to all, just as we *do* to you, so that He may establish your hearts blameless in holiness before our God and Father at the coming of our Lord Jesus Christ with all His saints."

MY BROTHER'S KEEPER

Loving one another *as Christ loved us* was His new commandment.[473] Likewise, loving one another has been the responsibility of all people for all time from the beginning of time. The tragic jealousy of Cain toward Abel motivated Adam's firstborn son to take the life of his second son. *"Then the LORD said to Cain, "Where is Abel your brother?" He said, "I do not know. Am I my brother's keeper?"*[474]

Jesus taught, *"For by your words you will be justified, and by your words you will be condemned."*[475] Cain's words convicted him of his brother's murder and are preserved in Scripture to remind all that we have a responsibility to one another.

James wrote, *"Brethren, if anyone among you wanders from the truth, and someone turns him back, let him know that he who turns a sinner from the error of his way will save a soul from death and cover a multitude of sins."*[476] What an important function of the church, to help those drawn away by sin to repent and be restored!

Being our brothers' and sisters' keeper also means we forgo liberties for their benefit. Paul wrote repeatedly about not eating meat and avoiding wine to keep others from stumbling.[477] We are also to focus our study on the gospel, not disputes over doubtful topics, especially with weak Christians or new converts.[478] In a time when meat was mainly available from markets supplied by pagan temples, partaking could lead immature Christians back into idolatry. How foolish to destroy the soul of one for whom Christ died for the sake of eating meat! How pointless to neglect the gospel and risk division over things the devil uses as distractions!

SUPPORT THOSE WHO UPHOLD THE TRUTH

Christianity is a way of life, The Way. Loving one another is the hallmark chosen by Christ for His church! *"By this all will know that you are My disciples, if you have love for one another."*[479] The New Testament is filled with examples and commands to edify and encourage one another in truth and good works through prayer and song, and by bearing one another's burdens. Yet, one of my favorite images of encouragement is in the Old Testament, Exodus 17, as Israel traveled toward Mt. Sinai. The Amalekites came out to wage war against God's people. Moses had Joshua lead the forces while Moses, Aaron, and Hur went to the mountaintop to overlook the battle. Moses stood with the rod of God raised in his hand, and Israel prevailed, but when Moses grew tired and his hands dropped, the

Amalekites prevailed. Aaron and Hur moved a stone to give Moses a place to sit and then stood to his left and to his right to hold up Moses' arms! They remained that way until the sun set, and Joshua's soldiers defeated the Amelikites.[480]

This account is preserved in Scripture for God's reasons. Clearly, the victory was not because of Joshua's military insight nor the strength of the Israelites on the battlefield. Moses held up the rod of God as he had been told to do at the Red Sea. God turned the battle, but He did not remove the work men had to do. We pray for His providence and are assured by His promises, but there is work for us to do. It is best done together.[481]

Therefore, Christians need to support one another, including our faithful church leaders. This is most important when our congregations are threatened by false teaching and apostasy.[482] We must prepare for such battles with Bible study and establish relationships that allow us to talk to one another about sin and error. Paul wrote, *"Now I myself am confident concerning you, my brethren, that you also are full of goodness, filled with all knowledge, able also to admonish one another."*[483] When false teaching threatens the church of Christ, we must know and submit to God's Word, so we can encourage and admonish others based on God's truth and not on friendships, family relationships, personalities, or positions.

ADMONISH THE ERRING

When your congregation is going through trials, some will join the defense, and others will be needed as encouragers. Carefully guard yourself against gossip, forming cliques, or other traps of the devil. Seek God's will through prayer and Bible study. Continue to do the work of the church and love one another.

We see the words *encourage*, *edify*, and *admonish* used for the work of supporting others as they learn, grow, and face trials. *Admonish* is also used for encouraging others to turn from sin. Remember that the same enemy that is attacking the faithful is winning the battle in the hearts of one who is championing false teaching or going back into a life of sin. We are to admonish and pray for a person who is in opposition that they may repent and be restored, speaking the truth in love.[484]

In 2 Thessalonians 3, Paul wrote that we are to withdraw fellowship from those who walk disorderly. That means not to keep company with a person who is going back into sin, so they may be ashamed, yet not to consider him or her an enemy. Instead, we are to admonish that person like a brother.[485] Withdrawing social interactions while going to that person to speak the truth in love can save a soul and the souls that person influences. We have careful guidelines for such conversations given in Matthew 18:15-20. These apply to a person caught up in any sin, not only false teaching.

If you find yourself in the position of needing admonishment to turn from sin or false doctrines, be humble. Do not be angry at the elder, brother, or sister who loves you and has the courage to come to you. They have been commanded by God to do so. Take courage. God says that you are not facing a temptation that others have not faced, and He will provide you a way of escape that you may be able to bear it.[486] When a fellow Christian comes to you or stands before you and teaches you the truth, he or she is showing your way of escape. Are you unsure what is right? Turn to God's Word and study with a desire to know God's will, not just looking for wording that might affirm your preconceptions.

Paul wrote to the Galatians who were being courted by false teachers. He reminded the Christians at Galatia that they had cared so much for him that if it had been possible, they would have plucked out their own eyes to give them to Paul who seems to have suffered terrible eye problems. Yet, in Paul's absence, they had begun listening to smooth-talking false teachers who had come into their midst, wanting the Galatians to be zealous toward them instead of God. Just so, the devil divides the body of Christ even today. Paul asked the Galatians, *"Have I therefore become your enemy because I tell you the truth?"*[487]

It is joyful work to edify others toward serving God, growing in their faith and obedience. Rebuking those in error is the tough side of admonishment. We are to love and support one another even if it costs our lives. Usually, we are only risking an awkward conversation. Sometimes we lose a relationship. Hopefully, we rescue a soul from death.[488] We are first to examine ourselves and address sin in our own lives.[489] We most certainly need to pray. We need to be ready to share scriptures that are pertinent to the sin that is endangering our sister or brother so that it is God's perfect will that we are offering and not a personal opinion.

SEVEN-POINT DISCUSSION GUIDE

1. False Teaching: Some people teach that sin and its consequences are manifestations of diseases, genetic traits, or innate disorders to suggest that a person cannot be held fully responsible for his or her choices. Yet, God who made us commands us not to be drunkards, not to participate in fornication or adultery, not to be given to violence, and not to doubt His judgment will come.

   How does this impact our responsibility to admonish one another?

In an old-fashioned fill-in-the-blanks format, complete the passages below. Each passage is from a New Testament example of edification and encouragement. Discuss what we learn from each.

2. Acts 4:36-37, "*And Joses, who was also named Barnabas by the apostles (which is translated Son of _____), a Levite of the country of Cyprus,* **having land, sold it, and brought the money and laid it at the apostles' feet**."[490]

3. Romans 16:3-4, "*Greet Priscilla and Aquila, my _____ in Christ Jesus, who* **risked their own necks for my life**, *to whom not only I give _____ , but also all the churches of the Gentiles.*"[491]

4. First John 3:16-17, "*By this we know love, because He laid down His life for us. And we also _____ to* **lay down our lives for the brethren**. *But* **whoever has this world's** _____ **, and sees his brother in need**, *and shuts up his heart from him, how does the love of God abide in him?*"[492]

5. Jude 3 *"Beloved, while I was very diligent to write to you concerning our common salvation, I found it necessary to write to you _____ _____ you to **contend earnestly for the faith** which was once for all delivered to the saints."*[493]

6. First Timothy 2:1-4, *"Therefore I _____ first of all that **supplications, prayers, intercessions, and giving of thanks be made for all men, for kings and all who are in authority**, that we may lead a quiet and peaceable life in all godliness and reverence. For this is good and acceptable in the sight of God our Savior, who desires all men to be saved and to come to the knowledge of _____."*[494]

7. Hebrews 10:24-25, *"And let us consider one another in order **to stir up love and good works, not forsaking the assembling of ourselves together**, as is the manner of some, but one another, and so much the more as you see the Day approaching."*[495]

CALL TO ACTION

Visit and send cards to shut-ins, the sick, *and* the erring. Include a note that encourages them to return to worship as soon as possible. Pray. Quickly call or visit those who do not attend worship. Do not shy away from discussing problems with a sister who is in danger of falling away. If you are not prepared on an issue, say so, and immediately seek the help of an elder or other mature Christian.

SONG OR PSALM

"LEAD ME TO SOME SOUL, TODAY"

PSALM 1:1–3
Blessed is the man
Who walks not in the counsel of the ungodly,
Nor stands in the path of sinners,
Nor sits in the seat of the scornful;
But his delight is in the law of the LORD,
And in His law he meditates day and night.
He shall be like a tree
Planted by the rivers of water,
That brings forth its fruit in its season,
Whose leaf also shall not wither;
And whatever he does shall prosper.[496]

SUGGESTED TOPIC FOR PRAYER
Pray for eyes to see those who need encouragement, courage to live like Christ, love to motivate obedience, and wisdom to discern and teach only God's truth.

LESSON 10

BE WORKERS

*"Let your light so shine before men,
that they may see your good works and glorify your Father in heaven."*

Matthew 5:16

Christ challenged His hearers to do what Israel was designed to do, shine! As a light, shine! As a city set on a hill, shine! Doing the works God sent them to do, shine! Glorifying God before the surrounding nations, shine!

Have you ever sat in a small chair with toddlers singing, "This little light of mine, I'm going to let it shine!"? How can we help but love those tiny fingers raised like candles in the air! Jesus said, *"Let your light so shine before men, that they may see your good works and glorify your Father in heaven."*[497] That is your memory verse. This Sunday school lesson is to shine by doing work that glorifies God.

BEE-ATTITUDE: PURPOSEFULLY DILIGENT

Sunflowers are well-named for their appearance and because young blooms track the sun from east to west each day. By morning, the blooms again face east to meet the rising sun because one side of the stem grows more rapidly in the day, and the other grows more rapidly at night. Sun-tracking increases plant growth, and warmer blooms attract more bees to fertilize sunflower seeds!

Likewise, worker bees are aptly named. Each year their diligence contributes to the production of 80% of food crops and produces 162 million pounds of honey in the U.S. alone. A worker bee assumes many responsibilities in her lifetime to keep the colony thriving. God designed every part of her tiny body to serve a purpose; to fly, navigate, locate food and water, gather pollen, sip nectar, make wax, shape honeycomb, clean the hive, make honey, feed larvae, produce royal jelly for queen bee larvae, release and perceive pheromones, communicate warnings and directions, warm the hive in cold weather, or protect the colony. Honeybees sleep in shifts, so hives stay as busy as...well, as busy as bees!

Sunflowers and bees evidence God's perfect design in creation. Yet, they lack sentience, the self-awareness that allows humans to wrestle with ideas like good and evil, purposeful existence, and an eternal destiny. You and I were created with eternal souls to prepare for eternity. The name Christian denotes one as a follower of Christ, God's Anointed. The word first used in Antioch meant literally "little-Christs." To be well-named, like Christ, we must live to glorify God. As Christian women, the inspired Scriptures reveal the perfect will of God for every aspect of our lives and the purposes God has for us in the family, community, and church. If we are to befit the name we wear, we must **diligently** seek and do His will![498]

PERFECT PLANS FOR DILIGENT WORKERS

Jesus Christ's last moments with His disciples before ascending to heaven were intense. Some had seen Him resurrected and witnessed to others who were hesitant to believe, so Jesus first rebuked them for the hardness of heart behind their disbelief. Then Jesus gave them their marching orders...His work to do. Mark records, *"And He said to them, "Go into all the world and preach the gospel to every creature. He who believes and is baptized will be saved; but he who does not believe will be condemned."*[499] Matthew records, *"And Jesus came and spoke to them, saying, "All authority has been given to Me in heaven and on earth. Go therefore and make disciples of all the nations, baptizing them in the name of the Father and of the Son and of the Holy Spirit, teaching them to observe all things that*

I have commanded you; and lo, I am with you always, even to the end of the age."[500] Followers of Christ are to preach the gospel and baptize believers.

Mark tells us that is just what they did! The truth of Christ's resurrection demanded it. *"So then, after the Lord had spoken to them, He was received up into heaven, and sat down at the right hand of God. And they went out and preached everywhere, the Lord working with them and confirming the word through the accompanying signs. Amen."*[501] Paul wrote that the message of the cross is the power of God to us who are being saved, but not like the Jewish scribes or Greek philosophers would have imagined. Man's wisdom, even in the 21st century, is far inferior to God's wisdom. God's purposeful design for saving man is to have men preach the truth to one another. *"For since, in the wisdom of God, the world through wisdom did not know God, it pleased God through the foolishness of the message preached to save those who believe."*[502]

In fact, even with Jesus directly involved in Saul's conversion, this work was not taken out of the disciples' hands. Jesus blinded Saul with a light from heaven and spoke to him on the road to Damascus. Saul asked Jesus, *"Lord, what do You want me to do?"*[503] Jesus did not answer the question by telling Saul to repent and be baptized but sent him to the house of Judas where he spent three days in prayer and fasting. Then, in a vision, Jesus sent Ananias to **heal Saul's blindness and baptize him into Christ**. Saul, who became known as the apostle Paul, spent the rest of his life doing this work of preaching and baptizing people into Christ. It is also our work is to teach and baptize believers as the church of Christ!

LADIES STILL DON'T PREACH!

Ladies don't preach. That is how God wants it according to Scripture,[504] and that is reason enough. Christian women do teach the Bible to children.[505] Older women are to teach younger women.[506] We support our husbands and other men as workers, deacons, preachers, teachers, or elders in the church.[507] We raise sons to teach and preach.[508] We financially support preachers and missionaries.[509] We assemble with the saints to hear and act on their messages.[510] We invite others to hear God's Word preached.[511] We kneel in prayer to ask God's direction, protection, and blessing on those who teach at home and in mission fields.[512] There is a lot of work for us to do, but it is not teaching men or otherwise exercising authority over men in the church.

We must not let the devil, the standards of this world, pride, or misdirected ambition lead us into conflict with our God. A woman in a pulpit or assuming eldership in a congregation may seem progressive to our society. She might teach with eloquence, dedication, a clear conscience, and a heartfelt calling. Still, it will not be to God's glory because it is against His will. Acting contrary to God's plan for His church is sin and will be judged as rebellion.

We are to be fellow workers, lights that shine in darkness. Dorcas knew how to shine! Dorcas's good works and charitable deeds were well-known in her community.[513] She ministered to the needs of others to God's glory and not her own. When she was dying, her neighbors appealed to the apostle Peter. When Peter raised Dorcas from the dead, the people of Joppa responded by believing in Christ!

The apostle Paul filled his epistles with tender greetings to those who supported him with their time, funds, prayers, and teaching of the gospel. He called these saints, both women and men, fellow workers: Priscilla and Aquila, Lydia, Clement, Onesimus, Philemon, Phoebe, Gaius, Timothy, Mary, Julia, Nereus and his sister, Titus, Silas, Luke, Euodia, Syntyche, and many others.[514] God certainly notices good works. In Hebrews, Paul writes, *"For God is not unjust to forget your work and labor of love which you have shown toward His name, in that you have ministered to the saints, and do minister."*[515] The blessing is in doing what God asks of us. By accepting our God-given roles, we please Him and show the world what it means to submit to God's will.

GOD'S WORKERS ARE NEVER IDLE

Several of Jesus' parables express the value of diligent work. Jesus said that His Father works, and He works.[516] God does not sleep.[517] He does not neglect or forget us.[518] He is never too busy to hear our prayers.[519] His arm is never shortened.[520] Nothing is too hard for the Lord.[521] Jesus promises to be with us until the end of the age.[522]

Christians are people of action motivated by belief in Christ.[523] We do not offer kind but empty words without action. Our action (work, obedience) makes an impact to God's glory. Jesus told of two sons who were told to work in their father's vineyard. One refused at first but repented and went to work in the vineyard. The other brother was quick to say he would go but never went to do the work. Jesus asked, *"Which of the two did the will of his father?"*[524] The sons represented the Jewish priests and elders who refused Jesus, the tax collectors, harlots, and other sinners who repented and believed in Him. The principle remains important. We cannot expect to build a house without wielding a hammer. We cannot glorify God without doing the work we are given.

Therefore, we need to get busy! We need to work with the diligence of the woman who lost a coin from her veil.[525] We need to be as determined as the good shepherd who went after the lost sheep.[526] We need to be as eager to see the kingdom grow as the prodigal son's father was to see his return.[527] God's Word says that if a person will not work he should not eat.[528] If one refuses to work in the kingdom, do you imagine that person will have a seat at the wedding banquet when Christ comes to receive His own?[529]

Women are encouraged in 1 Timothy to *"marry, bear children, manage the house, give no opportunity to the adversary to speak reproachfully."*[530] We are to lodge strangers, wash the saints' feet, relieve the afflicted, and follow every good work.[531] We are to aspire to lead a quiet life and work with our hands.

When people are not productively engaged, they will find something to do, often activities that do not serve God. Paul warned that young widows might be *"wandering about from house to house, and not only idle but also gossips and busybodies, saying things which they ought not"* (1 Timothy 5:13). Social media now removes the footwork. Widows do not have the corner on gossip, but the point is that we need to be about the Lord's work. Homemaking and raising a Christian family are undervalued, but the heartache and growing dysfunction in the world around us show the power of such a life. The devil seeks to destroy the family, marriage, the home, schools, and the church. Christian women have work to do with the promise, *". . . God is able to make all grace abound toward you, that you, always having all sufficiency in all things, may have an abundance for every good work."*[532]

FAITH BY WORKS

The first work we must do is believe.[533] When sincere belief in Christ directs our thoughts and actions, we have faith. Faith cannot be separated from obedience. We are to show our faith by our works. We are to shine![534] James wrote about showing faith by works. Extrabiblical texts tell us his knees were like a camel's knees from the hours he spent in prayer! Prayer itself is a work for Christ. In the church, works should be undertaken out of faith and love.

Our faith should drive our everyday work of caring for family and others. Faith gives our work a higher purpose and elevates it far above this world's foolish pursuits. Do you tend your garden or prepare meals for others? Do it unto God. Tell your children and grandchildren how food is a gift from God. Invite them to work alongside you while gardening or cooking. Glorify God's work in creation. Tell them of the great truths of Genesis 1:11-12, describing how a seed planted produces another plant just like itself. Choose good soil as you share the parable of the sower in the gospels.[535] Talk about every good thing as a gift from God.[536] Take a dish to someone who is shut-in or in need. Mail a church bulletin, tract, or card containing an encouraging Bible verse.[537] Bring a sister, child, or friend along so they can learn to do God's work, too.[538]

Give without expecting or accepting anything in return and you transform material things into heavenly treasure.[539] Be humble and do not seek recognition.[540] Ask God's blessings on your everyday work. Consider the widow's mite and Mary's pound of spikenard used to anoint Christ.[541] They have served as examples of loving sacrifice to God for 21 centuries![542]

Take courage in God's plan when you are challenged to do work you might not expect. You may need to take an aging or disabled relative into your home.[543] According to the Old and New Testaments, caring for grandparents, parents, orphans, or even a widowed aunt is our responsibility. The work can be a tremendous blessing for all involved if done lovingly and unto the Lord. It is not always easy to be a caregiver, but it is God's work. If this has not yet become your responsibility, you may offer to stay with someone who needs constant care, so their family can have a few hours to take care of other things or have a day away for respite. Some Christian couples do mighty works of service in foster care or by adopting a child.[544]

Sometimes, whole families develop relationships with a widowed neighbor or saint who needs help with errands, small repairs, or companionship. All these things are God's work.

WORKS REWARDED

Hebrews 6 contains assurances for those who diligently do the good works of God, who do not return to lives of sin. *"For God is not unjust to forget your work and labor of love which you have shown toward His name, in that you have ministered to the saints, and do minister. And we desire that each one of you show the same diligence to the full assurance of hope until the end, that you do not become sluggish, but imitate those who through faith and patience inherit the promises."* We can trust in this promised reward because it is impossible for God to lie and because Jesus Christ who gave Himself for us is seated at God's right hand! [545]

From His throne on high, Jesus Christ is quoted in Revelation 22:12 saying, *"And behold, I am coming quickly, and My reward is with Me, to give to every one according to his work."* On the Mount of Olives, Jesus described this for His disciples who asked about the end of the age. Read the familiar passage, and make notes about the work you do, even at home, that Jesus promises to reward.

MATTHEW 25:34-40

Then the King will say to those on His right hand, 'Come, you blessed of My Father, inherit the kingdom prepared for you from the foundation of the world:
for I was hungry and you gave Me food;
I was thirsty and you gave Me drink;
I was a stranger and you took Me in; I *was* naked and you clothed Me;
I was sick and you visited Me;
I was in prison and you came to Me.'

Then the righteous will answer Him, saying, 'Lord, when did we see You hungry and feed *You,* or thirsty and give *You* drink? When did we see You a stranger and take

> *You* in, or naked and clothe *You?* Or when did we see You sick, or in prison, and come to You?'
>
> And the King will answer and say to them, 'Assuredly, I say to you, inasmuch as you did *it* to one of the least of these My brethren, you did *it* to Me.'

Sweet sisters in Christ, shine! Shine here by doing works that care for God's children, bringing honor to the church and the name of Christ. Leave a sparkle in the hearts of those you touch so that they, too, will want to serve the Lord by serving, encouraging, supporting, teaching, and setting a godly example with a quiet life. Christ prophesied, *"Then the righteous will shine forth as the sun in the kingdom of their Father. He who has ears to hear, let him hear!"*[546] Shine by reflecting God's glory, now and forever!

SEVEN-POINT DISCUSSION GUIDE

1. False Teaching: Some people teach that, since we are saved by grace (Jesus' sacrifice) and not works of the law (Law of Moses), baptism is not essential to salvation. They call people who teach that we should obey all of Christ's commands 'legalists' or 'modern-day Pharisees. How did Christ contradict this in Matthew 28:18-20?

2. James says, *"But be doers of the word, and not hearers only, deceiving yourselves. For if anyone is a hearer of the word and not a doer, he is like a man observing his natural face in a mirror; for he observes himself, goes away, and immediately forgets what kind of man he was. But he who looks into the perfect law of liberty and continues in it, and is not a forgetful hearer but a doer of the work, this one will be blessed in what he does."*[547] What is a doer?

3. What work is he or she to do?

4. Where is the blessing?

5. James also asks, *"What does it profit, my brethren, if someone says he has faith but does not have works? Can faith save him? If a brother or sister is naked and destitute of daily food, and one of you says to them, "Depart in peace, be warmed and filled," but you do not give them the things which are needed for the body, what does it profit? Thus also faith by itself, if it does not have works, is dead."*[548] What does this tell us about feeding and clothing those in need?

6. Benevolence is used as an example by James. What else are we to do, knowing that *"faith by itself, if it does not have works, is dead"*?

7. Why do we do God's work?

CALL TO ACTION

With your sisters in Christ, make and prioritize a list of needs in the church or community. Share the list with elders or deacons. Let two or more women choose a task to do together, capitalizing on the opportunity to mentor others. Plan times to share progress, pray for the work, and see if additional help is needed. You might consider works of benevolence, visiting the sick and shut-in, prison ministries, preparing materials for the Bible school program, setting up Bible studies with new Christian women or younger women, planning activities for the youth to do for others, working in the church's library or work room to better organize teaching materials, training new Bible school teachers, gathering clothes and household for outreach programs, mailings to invite those in the community to worship, care of the building and grounds, etc.

SONG OR PSALM

"TO THE WORK"
"I WANT TO BE A WORKER FOR THE LORD"

PSALM 18:28–29
For You will light my lamp;
  *The L*ORD *my God will enlighten my darkness.*
For by You I can run against a troop,
  By my God I can leap over a wall.[549]

SUGGESTED TOPIC FOR PRAYER
Sometimes the needs of a hive shift, and worker bees must switch roles. Apologists, scientists who study bees, discovered that when worker bees change jobs, their brains stop aging. Do not draw back when you are faced with unexpected changes in your life or congregation. Sometimes you may realize that you need to change your life to align with God's will. Do not fear but pray for God to give you vitality of mind and body to meet the challenges you face. You will grow in your faith.

UNIT FOUR

BE KEEPERS OF THE FAITH

*Watch,
stand fast in the faith, be brave, be strong.
Let all that you do be done with love.*

1 Corinthians 16:13-14

UNIT FOUR INTRODUCTION

BE KEEPERS OF THE FAITH

Lessons 11-14 address our roles as we mature in Christ as keepers of The Faith, seeking to live worthily, faithfully, courageously, watchfully, and confidently. First consider, Sweet Sisters, who we are:

WE ARE PEOPLE OF THE FAITH.

"For I am not ashamed of the gospel of Christ, for it is the power of God to salvation for everyone who believes, for the Jew first and also for the Greek. For in it the righteousness of God is revealed from faith to faith; as it is written, "The just shall live by faith."[550]

WE WALK IN THE WAY.

*"Jesus said to him, "**I am the way**, the truth, and the life. No one comes to the Father except through Me."*[551]

*"So the word of the Lord grew mightily and prevailed… And about that time there arose a great commotion about **the Way**."*[552]

*" Therefore, brethren, having boldness to enter the Holiest by the blood of Jesus, by **a new and living way** which He consecrated for us, through the veil, that is, His flesh, and having a High Priest over the house of God, let us draw near with a true heart in full assurance of faith, having our hearts sprinkled from an evil conscience and our bodies washed with pure water."*[553]

WE ARE DISCIPLES OF CHRIST.

*"Now on the first day of the week, when **the disciples** came together to break bread, Paul, ready to depart the next day, spoke to them and continued his message until midnight."*[554]

WE ARE CHRISTIANS.
*"And when he had found him, he brought him to Antioch. So it was that for a whole year they assembled with the church and taught a great many people. And the disciples were first called **Christians** in Antioch."*[555]

WE ARE CHILDREN OF GOD.
*"Behold what manner of love the Father has bestowed on us, that **we should be called children of God**! Therefore the world does not know us, because it did not know Him. Beloved, now we are children of God; and it has not yet been revealed what we shall be, but we know that when He is revealed, we shall be like Him, for we shall see Him as He is. And everyone who has this hope in Him purifies himself, just as He is pure."*[556]

WE ARE SAINTS SET SPART FOR GOD'S PURPOSES.
"To the church of God which is at Corinth, to those who are sanctified in Christ Jesus, called to be saints, with all who in every place call on the name of Jesus Christ our Lord, both theirs and ours."[557]

WE ARE PILGRIMS TRAVELING HOME.
"Beloved, I beg you as sojourners and pilgrims, abstain from fleshly lusts which war against the soul, having your conduct honorable among the Gentiles, that when they speak against you as evildoers, they may, by your good works which they observe, glorify God in the day of visitation."[558]

WE ARE THE BRIDE AWAITING THE GROOM.
"Husbands, love your wives, just as Christ also loved the church and gave Himself for her, that He might sanctify and cleanse her with the washing of water by the word, that He might present her to Himself glorious church, not having spot or wrinkle or any such thing, but that she should be holy and without blemish."[559]

WE ARE THE CHURCH, AWAITING CHRIST.

"I thank my God always concerning you for the grace of God which was given to you by Christ Jesus, that you were enriched in everything by Him in all utterance and all knowledge, even as the testimony of Christ was confirmed in you, so that you come short in no gift, eagerly waiting for the revelation of our Lord Jesus Christ, who will also confirm you to the end, that you may be blameless in the day of our Lord Jesus Christ. God is faithful, by whom you were called into the fellowship of His Son, Jesus Christ our Lord."[560]

We are those who long to meet Jesus Christ. It is our hope to be counted worthy in Him.[561] We hope in Him because He loves and died for us, but was resurrected, overcoming death for all who are obedient to the gospel. We do not wait in fear but courageously prepare to meet our God. Should He return in our lifetimes, we want to be found faithful and watching for His return. We can be confident of salvation because Christ is our Savior and our Judge. God provides for us. He is absolutely able to keep those who are committed to Him!

LESSON 11

BE COUNTED WORTHY

*"You are witnesses, and God also,
how devoutly and justly and blamelessly we behaved ourselves
among you who believe;
as you know how we exhorted, and comforted,
and charged every one of you, as a father does his own children,
that you would walk worthy of God who calls you
into His own kingdom and glory."*

1 Thessalonians 2:10-12

We are created spiritual beings but live first in mortal bodies. We must rely on our God who is an eternal spirit to guide our walk. If a person is blind, light still exists, but he or she cannot perceive it. If deaf, sirens or music can fill the air but go equally unnoticed. Similarly, spiritual things exist beyond detection by our physical senses. Though a traffic light is unseen by a blind pedestrian, it still affects her safety, so she depends on other people, a guide dog, or adaptive devices for guidance. Our struggle to live righteous lives and avoid sin is part of a greater spiritual war being waged in heavenly places.[562] We must depend on God. In Him is all knowledge, goodness, truth, light, and love. Fulfilling God's plan to redeem us from spiritual death, Jesus Christ gave Himself to redeem our souls. The spiritual guidance we need to receive the grace of Jesus and walk worthy of God has been provided by the Holy Spirit in the Scriptures.

BEE-ATTITUDE: WORTHINESS

The Magna Carta of 1215 was the first of many treaties between England's rulers and its citizens. The treaty limited the powers of the king and assured certain rights to common people. Its influence has been far-reaching, including the property rights and assurance of trial by jury that are integral to the Constitution of the United States. Curiously, a subset of the Magna Carta's rules, the Charter of the Forest of 1225, gave commoners the right to harvest wild honey. The right to hunt and gather honey in the forests had previously been reserved for royalty.

Though earthly treaties may declare who is worthy to hold land or gather honey, God alone will determine whose name is in the Book of Life. Only in Christ and by the grace of God can we be counted worthy of salvation, but there are compelling passages that challenge us to live lives worthy of our calling.

WORTHINESS

Heavenly hosts praise God without ceasing. They sing *"Holy, Holy, Holy"* and *"You are worthy, Oh, Lord!"*[563] They laud Him as eternal, *"Holy, holy, holy, Lord God Almighty, Who was and is and is to come!"*[564] By inspiration, David sang, *"I will call upon the LORD, who is worthy to be praised; So shall I be saved from my enemies."*[565] The 24 elders foreseen in the Revelation fall before God's throne, declaring, *"You are worthy, O Lord, To receive glory and honor and power; For You created all things, And by Your will they exist and were created."*[566]

The 24 elders also extoll Christ as worthy in Revelation, calling Him the Lion of the Tribe of Judah and the Lamb that was slain when only He is found worthy to open the scroll with seven seals, *"You are worthy to take the scroll, and to open its seals; for You were slain, and have redeemed us to God by Your blood."*[567] Then, a hundred million heavenly creatures sing, *"Worthy is the Lamb who was slain to receive power and riches and wisdom, and strength and honor and glory and blessing!"*[568] After that, every creature of heaven and earth declares, *"Blessing and honor and glory and power be to Him who sits on the throne, and to the Lamb, forever and ever!"*[569]

GRACE

In Revelation 3:5, Christ promises faithful Christians, *"He who overcomes shall be clothed in white garments, and I will not blot out his name from the Book of Life; but I will confess his name before My Father and before His angels."*[570] During His earthly ministry, Christ described a wedding feast that a king prepared for his son. When the feast was ready, those who had been invited refused to come. In fury, the king sent his armies to destroy them and burn up their cities. He said, *"The wedding is ready, but those who were invited were not worthy."*[571] This parable was spoken to the Pharisees who did not believe Jesus and sought to kill Him. It revealed the fate of those who reject the Son of God.

Christ's parable continued with the king sending his servants into the highways and byways inviting everyone to the feast, filling the wedding hall with guests. However, a man came in without a wedding garment. When the king saw him, he sent him away to be cast into outer darkness where there would be weeping and gnashing of teeth.[572] The gospel invitation is to all, to Jews as well as Gentiles (non-Jews), to every nation. The man who came without a wedding garment was unprepared and speechless, without excuse. He was unworthy to be there for he was not clothed in Christ.

Paul wrote to Christians throughout Galatia, *"For you are all sons of God through faith in Christ Jesus. For as many of you as were baptized into Christ have put on Christ."*[573] Christ is the garment that clothes us and allows us to be counted worthy to come to the wedding feast, to be in the presence of the King. This is grace.

> *"But God, who is rich in mercy, because of His great love with which He loved us, even when we were dead in trespasses, made us alive together with Christ (by grace you have been saved), and raised us up together, and made us sit together in the heavenly places in Christ Jesus, that in the ages to come He might show the exceeding riches of His grace in His kindness toward us in Christ Jesus. For by grace you have been saved through faith, and that not of yourselves; it is the gift of God, not of works, lest anyone should boast. For we are*

> *His workmanship, created in Christ Jesus for good works, which God prepared beforehand that we should walk in them.*[574]

Worthy is God. Worthy is Christ. Loving us, our Holy, Holy, Holy Father sent His Son into the world so that the world through Him might be saved. We may be counted worthy by being in Christ. Outside of Christ, salvation is impossible for everyone. Jews who refuse to believe in God's Son and accept His authority are lost. Those who seek to come to the kingdom without putting on Christ are also lost. Yet the glory of God is that He by grace will make us, whether Jew or Gentile, alive in Christ.

> *"Grace to you and peace from God the Father and our Lord Jesus Christ, who gave Himself for our sins, that He might deliver us from this present evil age, according to the will of our God and Father, to whom be glory forever and ever. Amen."*[575]

OUR UNWORTHINESS

John the Baptist was an humble man in conduct, dress, and diet. He did not seek the approval of the religious leaders of his day. John explained his role to them, *"I baptize with water, but there stands One among you whom you do not know. It is He who, coming after me, is preferred before me, whose sandal strap I am not worthy to loose."*[576] Jesus said that *"among those born of women, there has not risen one greater than John the Baptist"* (Matthew 11:11). John did not seek his own glory but took great joy in the message he was sent to declare, *"Behold! The Lamb of God who takes away the sin of the world!"*[577] When his disciples told him that Jesus' disciples were baptizing more people than he, John assured them, *"He must increase, but I must decrease."*[578] John was a Messianic prophet, himself foretold by the prophet Isaiah[579] and the prophet Malachi in the last verses of the Old Testament.[580] By divine revelation, John understood that Jesus was the Christ.[581] As humbly and righteously as John lived, his role was to baptize the sinless Son of God and go before Him preaching repentance to prepare His way.[582]

In contrast to our sinless Lord, all men and women are unworthy, but not worthless. Peter was overwhelmed by the awareness of his own sinfulness when he witnessed the first miraculous catch of fish at Jesus' command. Realizing that he was in the presence of the Son of God, he fell to his knees. Our worth is that God created and loves us, and that Jesus loves and died for us.

Humility before Christ is a hallmark of faith. In Luke 7 a Roman centurion appealed to Jesus to heal a servant who was dear to him. He was a man who understood authority, commanding over 100 men within a legion of 6,000 soldiers. He sent Jewish friends to ask for Jesus' help, then sent others to intercept Him saying, *"Lord, do not trouble Yourself, for I am not worthy that You should enter under my roof. Therefore I did not even think myself worthy to come to You. But say the word, and my servant will be healed." Jesus marveled at his faith, "I say to you, I have not found such great faith, not even in Israel!"*[583] The centurion recognized Jesus' authority, calling Him Lord, and understood his own unworthiness based on his military experience. He deemed himself unworthy because he understood who Jesus is.

We are created beings. Our eternal God is the Creator, and Jesus Christ is the Word of God through whom everything was made. The prophet Isaiah wrote, *"But now, O Lord, You are our Father; We are the clay, and You our potter; And all we are the work of Your hand."*[584] We must humbly understand our relationship to the Creator. What else does Isaiah teach us about our relationship to the Creator with this imagery?

POTTER AND CLAY PASSAGES

Isaiah 29:16
Surely you have things turned around!
Shall the potter be esteemed as the clay;
For shall the thing made say of him who made it,
"He did not make me"?
Or shall the thing formed say of him who formed it,
"He has no understanding"?[585]

Isaiah 45:9
"Woe to him who strives with his Maker!
Let the potsherd *strive* with the potsherds of the earth!

Shall the clay say to him who forms it,
'What are you making?'
Or shall your handiwork *say*,
'He has no hands'? [586]

Isaiah 64:8
But now, O LORD, You *are* our Father;
We *are* the clay, and You our potter;
And all we *are* the work of Your hand. [587]

UNWORTHY BECAUSE OF SIN

Outside of Christ, we are unworthy to be in God's presence because of sin. In Jesus' parable of the prodigal son, the young man who wasted his father's money in riotous living came to his senses. He traveled home, planning his confession and plea for mercy. *"And the son said to him, 'Father, I have sinned against heaven and in your sight, and am no longer worthy to be called your son.'"* [588] Instead of rebuke, he found his father watching and waiting for his return. Sin is doing things that are against God the Father's will. Like the younger son, when we repent and confess our sins, we are received by our Heavenly Father with open arms and restored to full sonship.

The older brother in this parable was unwilling to forgive his brother. The father went out to him, too. He encouraged him to rejoice that his brother was returned from the dead. When we live in sin and do evil works rather than the works of God, we are lost. When we refuse to forgive others, we cannot be forgiven and are lost. Either way, we are separated from God, dead in sin. The devil convinces some people that they can never make things right with God, but this is not so. Jesus who died for us is also our judge. Will He not judge righteous judgment? Our Heavenly Father will welcome home those who repent and come home to do His will! We are not worthy if we are found trusting in the things of this world, refusing to repent of sin, rejecting Christ, and living in rebellion against God. Examine the passages in the table, and note what makes us "not worthy" of Christ.

PASSAGES ON BEING WORTHY OF GRACE OR PUNISHMENT

Luke 3:8
(John the Baptist speaking to the Pharisees) "Therefore bear fruits worthy of repentance, and do not begin to say to yourselves, 'We have Abraham as *our* father.' For I say to you that God is able to raise up children to Abraham from these stones."

Matthew 10:34-37
(Jesus speaking) "Do not think that I came to bring peace on earth. I did not come to bring peace but a sword. For I have come to *'set a man against his father, a daughter against her mother, and a* daughter-in-law *against her* mother-in-law'; and *'a man's enemies will be those of his own household.'* He who loves father or mother more than Me is not worthy of Me. And he who loves son or daughter more than Me is not worthy of Me."

Matthew 10:38-39
(Jesus speaking) "And he who does not take his cross and follow after Me is not worthy of Me. He who finds his life will lose it, and he who loses his life for My sake will find it."

Hebrews 10:28-31
"Anyone who has rejected Moses' law dies without mercy on the testimony of two or three witnesses. Of how much worse punishment, do you suppose, will he be thought worthy who has trampled the Son of God underfoot, counted the blood of the covenant by which he was sanctified a common thing, and insulted the Spirit of grace? For we know Him who said, *"Vengeance is Mine, I will repay,"* says the Lord. And again, *"The Lord will judge His*

people." It is a fearful thing to fall into the hands of the living God."

WALKING WORTHILY

Walking worthy of Christ is a great way to live! You will be busy. You will have purpose. You won't worry about material things. You will see the people around you as the children of God, not as your rivals or competitors. There won't be much "me time," but you will be exceedingly beautiful in the eyes of the Lord. If you have a husband, he will value you most for your spirit and godliness.

Paul repeatedly wrote to the churches about walking worthily, *"Walk worthy of God who calls you into His own kingdom and glory."*[589] He wrote to the Colossian Christians, defining walking worthily, *"For this reason we also, since the day we heard it, do not cease to pray for you, and to ask that you may be filled with the knowledge of His will in all wisdom and spiritual understanding; that you may walk worthy of the Lord, fully pleasing Him, being fruitful in every good work and increasing in the knowledge of God; strengthened with all might, according to His glorious power, for all patience and longsuffering with joy; giving thanks to the Father who has qualified us to be partakers of the inheritance of the saints in the light."*

Reread carefully to complete the close statements:

   a. We need knowledge of God's will, and all His _____ and spiritual _____ . These are sought through _____ .
   b. We please the Lord by being fruitful in every good _____ and by increasing in the knowledge of _____ .
   c. We have God to give us strength and _____ when we do suffer for Christ.
   d. We are to find _____ and be _____ even in trials.
   e. The Father has qualified us, made us worthy, to share in the _____ _____ of the saints in the light, salvation.

Paul taught that walking worthily affects how we treat one another. He wrote from prison to the Ephesian church, *"I, therefore, the prisoner of the Lord, beseech you to walk worthy of the calling with which you were called, with all lowliness and gentleness, with longsuffering, bearing with one another in love, endeavoring to keep the unity of the Spirit in the bond of peace. There is one body and one Spirit, just as you were called in one hope of your calling; one Lord, one faith, one baptism; one God and Father of all, who is above all, and through all, and in you all.*"[590] The Apostle Paul encouraged the churches in letters addressed to Rome, Philippi, Colossae, and Thessalonica to be united, support those who did mission work, and be fruitful in every good work to walk worthy of the gospel of Christ.[591]

WORTHWHILE

Paul wrote to the Ephesians, *"See then that you walk circumspectly, not as fools but as wise, redeeming the time, because the days are evil. Therefore do not be unwise, but understand what the will of the Lord is."*[592] One tool for in-depth Bible study is a commentary. Coffman[593] writes that "*Redeeming the time*" means "buying up the opportunities," "taking advantage of all occasions for doing good," etc.[594] We redeem the time by doing God's work even when we live in times of evil. We can encourage one another to walk worthily in *"psalms and hymns and spiritual songs, singing and making melody in your heart to the Lord, giving thanks always for all things to God the Father in the name of our Lord Jesus Christ, submitting to one another in the fear of God."*

Sisters, here Paul brings us back to our responsibility to submit to our husbands, *"Therefore, just as the church is subject to Christ, so let the wives be to their own husbands in everything."*[595] When we are submissive in human relationships we learn and show the relationship of Christians to God, setting aside our will to do His will, for He alone is worthy!

Coffman also connects the idea of *"redeeming the time for the days are evil"* to the terrible persecution that came with the destruction of Jerusalem in A.D. 70. The Apostles and others were already experiencing significant threats, abuse, and even death at the hands Jews, Greeks, and Romans. Their response was to rejoice to be counted worthy to suffer persecution for the name of Christ. Acts 5:41 records, *"So they departed from the presence of the council, rejoicing that they were counted worthy to suffer shame for His name."* Paul wrote, *"For I consider that the sufferings of this present time are not worthy of being compared with the glory which shall be revealed in us."*[596]

CONCLUSION

Two thousand years later, Christians continue to endure persecution all over the world. In Luke 21:33-36, Jesus said of the end of time, *"Heaven and earth will pass away, but My words will by no means pass away. But take heed to yourselves, lest your hearts be weighed down with carousing, drunkenness, and cares of this life, and that Day come on you unexpectedly. For it will come as a snare on all those who dwell on the face of the whole earth. Watch therefore, and pray always that you may be counted worthy to escape all these things that will come to pass, and to stand before the Son of Man."* Being counted worthy to escape persecution does not mean that we will not experience it but that when it comes, we may faithfully endure it.

Paul asks in Romans, *"Who shall separate us from the love of Christ? Shall tribulation, or distress, or persecution, or famine, or nakedness, or peril, or sword? As it is written: "For Your sake, we are killed all day long; We are accounted as sheep for the slaughter." Yet in all these things we are more than conquerors through Him who loved us. For I am persuaded that neither death nor life, nor angels nor principalities nor powers, nor things present nor things to come, nor height nor depth, nor any other created thing, shall be able to separate us from the love of God which is in Christ Jesus our Lord."*[597]

APPLICATION IN OUR LIVES

Though we cannot earn salvation, our lives must be lived to the glory of our Lord. We are to be *"zealous of good works"* (see Titus 2:11–14, below). The Oxford Dictionary defines *zeal* as "great energy or enthusiasm in pursuit of a cause or an objective." If your cause is Christ's Kingdom, what good works are you undertaking with great energy and enthusiasm? If you are not yet doing so, where might you begin?

> "For the grace of God that brings salvation has appeared to all men, teaching us that, denying ungodliness and worldly lusts, we should live soberly, righteously, and godly in the present age, looking for the blessed hope and glorious appearing of our great God and Savior

Be Counted Worthy

Jesus Christ, who gave Himself for us, that He might redeem us from every lawless deed and purify for Himself His own special people, zealous for good works."[598]

SEVEN-POINT DISCUSSION GUIDE

1. False Teaching: Some people teach that good people, even if they are not obedient to Christ's gospel, will go to heaven because God would not condemn a good person to hell.

    If being a "good person" were enough, why did God send Jesus to die in our place?

    "In Him we have redemption through His blood, the forgiveness of sins, according to the riches of His grace."[599]

    (Christ) "who Himself bore our sins in His own body on the tree, that we, having died to sins, might live for righteousness—by whose stripes you were healed."[600]

2. It is common for political rhetoric, commercials, and greeting cards to flatter the audience by saying, "You deserve ..." This is dangerous thinking that urges the listener toward pride, selfishness, and coveting whatever the vendor is selling and things that rightfully belong to others.

    What does God's Word say we deserve (without Christ)?

    "And the LORD God commanded the man, saying, "Of every tree of the garden you may freely eat; but of the tree of the knowledge of good and evil you shall not eat, for in the day that you eat of it you shall surely die."[601]

    "For the wages of sin is death, but the gift of God is eternal life in Christ Jesus our Lord."[602]

    "for all have sinned and fall short of the glory of God"[603]

3. From the sinning of Adam and Eve in the Garden, God began gradually revealing His plan of reconciliation. Our Holy God came in the flesh as Jesus Christ to pay the price for our sins. He died a death He did not deserve, that we by His grace might live eternally in His presence.

　"Jesus said to him, "I am the way, the truth, and the life. No one comes to the Father except through Me."[604]

　"Nor is there salvation in any other, for there is no other name under heaven given among men by which we must be saved."[605]

　"He who has the Son has life; he who does not have the Son of God does not have life."[606]

4. Proverbs 25:16 cautions the man or woman of God,

　"Have you found honey?
　Eat only as much as you need,
　Lest you be filled with it and vomit."

　What might this indelicate statement mean about self-indulgence in the pleasures of this life?

5. Consider Galatians 3:26-27, "For you are all sons of God through faith in Christ Jesus. For as many of you as were baptized into Christ have put on Christ."[607]

　How do we "put on Christ"?

　Is **faith** in Christ separate from **obedience** to Christ?

6. Ephesians 2:4-10 is an inspired explanation of God's grace toward us.

　"But God, who is rich in mercy, because of His great love with which
　He loved us, even when we were dead in trespasses, made us alive

*together with Christ (**by grace you have been saved**), and raised us up together, and made us sit together in the heavenly places in Christ Jesus, that in the ages to come He might show the exceeding riches of His grace in His kindness toward us in Christ Jesus. For **by grace you have been saved through faith**, and that not of yourselves; it is **the gift of God, not of works**, lest anyone should boast. For **we are His workmanship, created in Christ Jesus for good works**, which God prepared beforehand that we should walk in them.*[608]

Who makes us worthy of salvation?

When we walk worthily, what are we created in Christ to do?

7. Walking worthily includes doing good works with zeal!

    Think of a person's inspiring example of zeal from Scripture or the life of a Christian who encourages you by example. Describe his or her zealous works and how they glorify God.

BE KEEPERS

SONG OR PSALM

"I WILL CALL UPON THE LORD"

PSALM 118
I will love You, O Lord, my strength.
The Lord is my rock and my fortress and my deliverer;
My God, my strength, in whom I will trust;
My shield and the horn of my salvation, my stronghold.
I will call upon the Lord, who is worthy to be praised;
So shall I be saved from my enemies.[609]

SUGGESTED TOPIC FOR PRAYER

Pray to be counted worthy, to see opportunities to do good works that are worthy of the name of Christ.

LESSON 12

BE DEEMED COURAGEOUS

*"For God has not given us a spirit of fear,
but of power and of love and of a sound mind."*

2 Timothy 1:7

Jesus commanded, *"Fear not."* Christ was preparing His disciples for the persecutions they would face. His command is also important in lesser trials. When a study of the Gospels first made me aware that Jesus commands us to fear not, I caught myself excusing my own inaction by saying, "I was afraid that...." I was afraid that I could not get there in time. I was concerned that I could not do a good job. I was worried that I might offend someone. Different wording, but the same shortcoming. Fear and its cousin, worry, erode our trust in God and can keep us from doing the work we are sent to do. Fear is the opposite of faith. Before He calmed the sea of Galilee, Jesus asked His Apostles, *"Why are you fearful, O you of little faith?"*[610]

Jesus also said we should spread the gospel without fear of men but fearing God. *"Are not two sparrows sold for a copper coin? And not one of them falls to the ground apart from your Father's will. But the very hairs of your head are all numbered. Do not fear therefore; you are of more value than many sparrows."*[611] The epistles of Peter, John, and Paul reiterate the importance of not yielding to fear of men. Paul had suffered much for the

Lord when he wrote, *"God has not given us a spirit of fear, but of power and of love and of a sound mind."* Christian women take courage in God's strength.

BEE-ATTITUDE: COURAGE

Worker honeybees die after stinging someone because their stingers are barbed and tear away with part of their abdomen. They only sting under great duress since it is a life-ending choice. If a hive is threatened, the bees first make a tremendous buzzing sound to frighten the intruder away. This warning sound is so effective that hives are located along fence rows in Africa to keep elephants off farmland. When an elephant pushes against a fence, the beehives are rocked, and the buzzing that follows causes the enormous mammal to retreat. African elephants will retreat and sound a distinct warning call for "beware the buzzing bees!" Not even a pachyderm wants to be swarmed by angry bees. The collective courage of the honeybee colony protects the hive, saves farmers' crops from trampling, and removes one major reason elephants are hunted.

Christian women must also be courageous in times of trial. Our defense is the gospel. We have the assurance of God's power and promises. We take courage from fellowship with faithful brethren. We pray. We encourage one another. We are His church. He tells us, *"Do not fear."*[612] Like the bees that send a herd of elephants running, the Holy Spirit promises that if we resist the devil, he will flee from us.[613] The gates of hell will not prevail against the church of Christ.[614] His Word will not pass away.[615] Jesus died to redeem us and awaits us in Glory with the crown of life.[616]

TRUST GOD'S STRENGTH: SAMSON

During the period when judges governed Israel, Samson's birth was foretold to his parents with the command that he would be a Nazarite from the womb to the grave. Neither his mother nor he ate or drank of the grapevine and no razor touched his head. Samson judged Israel for 20 years and was known for incredible physical strength. Samson fell in love with a Philistine woman and asked his parents to secure her to be his wife. Unbeknownst to them, God was using Samson to move against the Philistines. Though displeased, his parents conceded and journeyed with him to meet the woman. Judges 14 says,

> "So Samson went down to Timnah with his father and mother, and came to the vineyards of Timnah. Now to his surprise, a young lion came roaring against him. And the Spirit of the Lord came mightily upon him, and he tore the lion apart as one would have torn apart a young goat, though he had nothing in his hand. But he did not tell his father or his mother what he had done.
>
> Then he went down and talked with the woman; and she pleased Samson well. After some time, when he returned to get her, he turned aside to see the carcass of the lion. And behold, a swarm of bees and honey were in the carcass of the lion. He took some of it in his hands and went along, eating. When he came to his father and mother, he gave some to them, and they also ate. But he did not tell them that he had taken the honey out of the carcass of the lion.
> So his father went down to the woman. And Samson gave a feast there, for young men used to do so. And it happened, when they saw him, that they brought thirty companions to be with him. Then Samson said to them, "Let me pose a riddle to you. If you can correctly solve and explain it to me within the seven days of the feast, then I will give you thirty linen garments and thirty changes of clothing. But if you cannot explain it to me, then you shall give me thirty linen garments and thirty changes of clothing." And they said to him, "Pose your **riddle**, that we may hear it."
>
> So he said to them: "Out of the eater came something to eat, And out of the strong came something sweet." Now for three days they could not explain the riddle."[617]

The Philistines threatened Samson's wife and said they would kill her and her father if she did not get the answer to Samson's riddle for them. She wept and pressed Samson for seven days until he revealed the answer to his riddle. A series of violent conflicts followed with many Philistines dying at the hands of Samson.

Eventually, the infamous Delilah seduced Samson to reveal the source of his strength and cut his hair as he slept. This led to his capture by the Philistines who blinded Samson and imprisoned him. When the nobility of the Philistines gathered to celebrate Samson's defeat, guards stood him between the pillars in the temple of their false god, Dagon. There Samson prayed for God to restore his strength. God enabled him to pull the pillars down, killing more Philistines at his death than in his life and showing their idol to be an impotent lie.

God gave Samson such strength that he could kill the young lion with his bare hands. God restored Samson's strength when Samson stood chained between the pillars of a pagan temple. In weakness and humiliation, Samson turned to God and found victory. We cannot always trust our perception of things. We may think we are being shrewd but only invite sin. What we desire most can be used to our detriment as were the Philistine women in Samson's life. God must be our strength. His Word must be our source of wisdom. When we are weak but trust in God, we know true strength.[618]

FEAR GOD

Even though God first loved us, His judgment is sure against those who refuse to believe and obey Him. There is coming a day when we will all come before the throne to be judged by our actions, our every word, and how we have treated one another. God is merciful, but His judgment is just and final. For this reason, we are right to fear Him. He will not judge us with different standards based on wealth, worldly achievements, excuses, or hardships. We will receive neither leniency nor harsher judgment because of our nationality, race, gender, enslavement, or family name. God is not a respecter of persons. Yet Christians can boldly come before His throne in prayer and will be able to stand before Him on the Day of Judgment because we are in Christ who is worthy.

Fear of God should motivate us to obey His commands. *"By faith Noah, being divinely warned of things not yet seen, moved with godly fear, prepared an ark for the saving of his household, by which he condemned the world and became heir of the righteousness which is according to faith."*[619] Some denominational doctrines discourage people from being baptized, encourage baptism of infants who cannot yet believe or confess Christ and who have no sin, or deny baptism's role in our salvation and teach that baptism is to outwardly show men their inward faith. If we fear God, we will not yield to these false doctrines. It is my loving prayer that those who seek to serve God but have been taught error will have their hearts and eyes opened and obey our Lord.

Look at God's Word for yourself: Baptism is commanded by Jesus Christ.[620] In baptism we are buried, putting to death the old life we led in sin.[621] In baptism, the blood of Christ cleanses us of our sins.[622] We are lifted from the watery grave of baptism to walk in newness of life, recreated to life in Him.[623]

Some people accept false teachings because it fits the way they already think. Consider the lesson taught by the account of Naaman who sought cleansing from leprosy from the prophet Elisha. Naaman had expectations that were not met. He did not understand why Elisha did not come out to meet him but only sent a servant. He did not like being told to wash seven times in the Jordan river. At first Naaman relied on his own thinking. He was about to head back to Syria with his leprosy, but those who loved him persuaded Naaman to do just what the prophet told him to do. After that seventh dip his skin was restored like the skin of a baby!

Some people accept false teachings because it fits the way others want them to think and cave to social pressures. Haven't you heard people question God's requirement of baptism with hypotheticals? "Baptism can't be necessary. What if a young woman believed and repented but was hit by a falling brick on the way to the baptistry? Would God not save her?" Perhaps you have heard others rely on 'what the preacher told them.' Consider 1 Kings 13: 1- 34, an account of a prophet from Judah who was sent to prophecy against Israel, but cautioned by the Lord, *"You shall not eat bread, nor drink water, nor return by the same way you came."*[624]

The young prophet delivered the message of the Lord, resisted the king's invitation, and headed home another way. Yet, when a prophet from Israel sought him out and lied saying that an angel had told him to take the young prophet home and feed him, he accepted the invitation. God's judgment came as they sat at the table, *"'Because you have disobeyed the word of the* Lord, *and have not kept the commandment which the* Lord *your*

God commanded you, but you came back, ate bread, and drank water in the place of which the Lord *said to you, "Eat no bread and drink no water," your corpse shall not come to the tomb of your fathers."*[625] This came to be that very day. We must obey God in belief, repentance, confession of Christ, and baptism. We must not be led astray by people who claim to have new insights or even messages from angels.[626]

Some discount baptism as a work and imagine it detracts from grace, but baptism is obedience to God and necessary for salvation. His Word never sets obedience in opposition to grace. When the Bible speaks against the works of the Law, it is addressing the desire of Judaizers who wanted to bind the Mosaic Law on Gentile Christians. Doing so would have denied the power of Jesus' death on the cross, the sacrifice that fulfilled the Old Law and initiated a New Testament.[627] We submit to baptism, but even the physical act is done to us. Someone else lowers us into the water and lifts us up from the water. Salvation is accomplished by the cleansing of Christ's blood, not by bathing ourselves.[628] Salvation is still wholly a gift of grace in Christ because His death, burial, and resurrection made our salvation possible.[629]

At Pentecost, believing Jews who learned they had executed the Son of God cried, *"What shall we do?"* and Peter answered as Christ had commanded the apostles, *"Repent, and let every one of you be baptized in the name of Jesus Christ for the remission of sins; and you shall receive the gift of the Holy Spirit. For the promise is to you and to your children, and to all who are afar off, as many as the Lord our God will call."*[630] Peter's answer to their question was the same answer given when Cornelius and the Philippian jailer asked the same question, afar off as Gentiles.[631] The answer was the same for the churches of Asia, afar off by distance.[632] The answer is the same for us today, though we are afar off in time. When we confess our belief in Jesus Christ, repent of sin, and are immersed in baptism, we receive the gift of the Holy Spirit, which is eternal life.[633]

Peter later wrote that Noah's delivery in the ark was a type for the antitype of *"baptism which now saves us."*[634] Examine the great commission given by our Lord just before His ascension into heaven and make notes.

MATTHEW 28: 18-20

And **Jesus** came and spoke to them, saying, "All authority has been given to Me in heaven and on earth.

Go therefore and (a) **make disciples of all the nations,** (b) **baptizing them in the name of the Father and of the Son and of the Holy Spirit,** (c) **teaching them to observe all things that I have commanded you;**

and (d) lo, I am with you always, *even* to the end of the age." Amen.[635]

NOTES

Who spoke?

By whose authority?

Telling his disciples to do what?

a.

b.

c.

Promising what?

d.

The sacrifice of Jesus Christ for our sins reconciles us to God. The conscience is purified by Christ because our sins are washed away when our physical bodies are baptized at His command and into His death, washed in water but purified by our Savior's

blood. "Therefore, brethren, having boldness to enter the Holiest by the blood of Jesus, by a new and living way which He consecrated for us, through the veil, that is, His flesh, and having a High Priest over the house of God, let us draw near with a true heart in full assurance of faith, having our hearts sprinkled from an evil conscience and our bodies washed with pure water."[636] Obedience to baptism does not negate the grace of Christ but accepts it in obedience to His commands.

The New Testament contains the four Gospels that record the life of Christ, the book of Acts that records the establishment and spread of the church of Christ, epistles (letters) written by the apostles and disciples to the churches, and the prophetic book of Revelation. All are inspired Scripture, recorded by men with the guidance of the Holy Spirit. Some false teachers use this delineation to say that baptism is only described in Acts (The Acts of the Apostles), classifying it as a non-binding book of history. They then call the epistles, written by the same inspired Apostles and disciples, books of doctrine. The error of this human doctrine is teaching that we should look only to books of 'doctrine' to decide 'doctrinal matters.' Relegation of inspired scriptures as irrelevant by assigning Acts a genre' classification of history is a device of false teaching.[637] We are not to believe a lie.[638] The suggestion of a discrepancy in the practices of the early church as recorded in Acts and the later teachings of the Apostles is also false.

For clarity, there is no conflict between the history of baptism in conversions described in Acts and the doctrine taught in the epistles.[639] In Acts, the disciple, Luke, recorded numerous examples of conversions where Peter, Ananias, Phillip, Paul, and others preached and baptized believers for the remission of sins in Christ. Baptism for the remission of sins was clearly practiced by the inspired Apostles and Spirit-filled evangelists in Acts. The epistles were letters written by the same Paul, Peter, and John (plus James and Jude) to the same churches whose establishment is described in Acts.

The doctrine that baptism is not taught in the epistles is also false. In Colossians, Paul cautioned the early church to *"Beware lest anyone cheat you through philosophy and empty deceit, according to the tradition of men, according to the basic principles of this world, and not according to Christ."*[640] Therefore, it is our responsibility to examine the epistles. Hebrews 6:1–3 specifies **baptism** in a list of the elementary principles of Christ, *"repentance from dead works and of faith toward God, of the doctrine of baptisms, of laying on of hands, of the resurrection of the dead, and eternal judgment."*[641] Paul wrote to the Ephesians of **"one Lord, one faith, one baptism,**[642]**"** to the Colossians of being **"buried with Him in baptism"** and **"raised with Him through faith in the working of God,"**[643] and to Corinth saying, **"For by one Spirit we were all baptized into one body**—*whether Jews or Greeks, whether slaves or free—and have all been made to drink into one Spirit."*[644] The false doctrine of differentiating Acts from the epistles on doctrinal matters is **not** supported by God's Word. The epistles, the book of Acts, the very words of Christ recorded in the Gospels, and the book of Revelation all teach baptism.[645]

We are baptized for the same reason that we obey in all things: because we love and fear God. Paul told the Philippians to *"work out your own salvation with fear and trembling."*[646] He wrote to the Hebrews, *"Therefore we must give the more earnest heed to the things we have heard, lest we drift away. For if the word spoken through angels proved steadfast, and every transgression and disobedience received a just reward, how shall we escape if we neglect so great a salvation, which at the first began to be spoken by the Lord, and was confirmed to us by those who heard Him, God also bearing witness both with signs and wonders, with various miracles, and gifts of the Holy Spirit, according to His own will?"* [647]

LOVE CASTS OUT FEAR

When we are living as God wills, the fear of God works to keep us faithful. Our hope of eternal life is founded on Christ and promised to the faithful by our God who does not lie. Christ said, *"Do not fear, little flock, for it is your Father's good pleasure to give you the kingdom"* (Luke 12:32). John's Gospel and letters draw our attention to the love of God. He wrote, *"Love has been perfected among us in this: that we may have boldness in the day of judgment; because as He is, so are we in this world. There is no fear in love; but perfect love casts out fear because fear involves torment. But he who fears has not been made perfect in love. We love Him because He first loved us."* [648] This is not a contradiction, but an assurance for the faithful child of God who has *"received the Spirit of adoption by whom we cry out, 'Abba, Father.'"* [649]

In times of trial, we must remember the love of God but also hold Him in reverence and awe. Sometimes hardships result from our own sins as God disciplines us, much like a human father disciplines a child he loves.[650] Experiencing God's chastening without understanding can lead to a feeling of hopelessness or rebellion. Hebrews 12:11 says, *"Now no chastening seems to be joyful for the present, but painful; nevertheless, afterward it yields the peaceable fruit of righteousness to those who have been trained by it."* [651] Proverbs says that a parent who loves his son disciplines him promptly.[652]

Receiving discipline with fear and respect for God is critical to remaining faithful and gaining spiritual maturity. Proverbs also cautions us that, *"He who hates correction will die."* [653] When God grants us forgiveness of sins, we do not always avoid earthly consequences of our actions. A person might truly repent for stealing something and be forgiven by God, yet still answer to civil courts for the crime. Repentance over divorcing a spouse without scriptural grounds (adultery) can gain God's forgiveness for the sins involved, but no Scripture states that it frees one to remarry. We must not allow the devil to use such occasions to seed our hearts with resentment or rebellion. Our eternal lives are at stake. When we love God and fear Him, we will not allow our emotions to drive us away from Him in seasons of rebuke. Seasons of refreshing will come.[654] We become strengthened and learn patience in the fight against sin by the lessons God delivers.

DO NOT FEAR MAN

When Jesus was crucified, His apostles scattered. Only John, Mary the mother of Jesus, her sister, and two other women are mentioned as standing nearby the cross. We are told that a council member, Joseph of Arimathea, took courage and asked Pilate for the body of Jesus, then buried Him in his own tomb.[655] Nicodemus, a Pharisee, brought a hundred pounds of myrrh and aloes to prepare Jesus' body for burial.[656] They knew they were in danger from the Jewish leaders who were their colleagues and the Romans who ruled, but their love of Jesus was more powerful. It must be so for us, too, or the devil will use our fear to destroy our faith.

When the Jews commanded the apostles not to teach in Jesus' name, they declared, *"We ought to obey God rather than man."* We can quote the psalmist, *"The LORD is my helper; I will not fear. What can man do to me?"*[657] Read and annotate 2 Timothy 1:7-14 below, looking for why we do not fear man or physical death.

2 TIMOTHY 1:7-14
PAUL'S FINAL LETTER FROM PRISON
AS HE AWAITED EXECUTION.

For God has not given us a spirit of fear, but of power and of love and of a sound mind.

Therefore do not be ashamed of the testimony of our Lord, nor of me His prisoner, but share with me in the sufferings for the gospel according to the power of God,

who has saved us and called *us* with a holy calling, not according to our works, but according to His own purpose and grace which was given to us in Christ Jesus before time began,

but has now been revealed by the appearing of our Savior Jesus Christ, *who* has abolished death and brought life and immortality to light through the gospel, to which I was appointed a preacher, an apostle, and a teacher of the Gentiles.

For this reason I also suffer these things; nevertheless I am not ashamed, for I know whom I have believed and am persuaded that He is able to keep what I have committed to Him until that Day.

Hold fast the pattern of sound words which you have heard from me, in faith and love which are in Christ Jesus.

That good thing which was committed to you, keep by the Holy Spirit who dwells in us.[658]

Hebrews 11 and 12 are wholly dedicated to addressing faith, courage, and endurance. Read them carefully, reflect verse by verse. When we enjoy living in times of freedom and abundance, we are easily distracted from spiritual matters. Use times of relative peace to prepare for trials. Study to gain understanding of God's chastening and the proving of your faith so that when trials come, you do not fall away under duress.

Pray in faith for what you need when trials come. Smaller difficulties prepare us for greater challenges. The example of our Lord Jesus in His tribulation anchors our faith. The Gospel of Luke records many occasions when Jesus withdrew to solitude to pray, including the night He was betrayed. The Apostle Paul was called to suffer great things for Jesus' sake.[659] His letters to Philippi, Ephesus, Colossae, and Philemon were written while he was imprisoned, yet are filled with encouragement, thanks, and prayers for the churches.

Most scholars believe Paul was the author of Hebrews. The book was first written to Jewish Christians who were scattered by persecution. It uses Old Testament symbols to help Christians understand how the sacrifice of Christ and His church are a better covenant (testament) than the Law of Moses that they no longer practiced. The same is true for you and me because we "*have come to Mount Zion and to the city of the living God, the heavenly Jerusalem, to an innumerable company of angels, to the general assembly and church of the firstborn who are registered in heaven, to God the Judge of all, to the spirits of just men made perfect, to Jesus the Mediator of the new covenant, and to the blood of sprinkling that speaks better things than that of Abel.*" "*... Since we are receiving a kingdom which cannot be shaken, let us have grace, by which we may serve God acceptably with reverence and godly fear. For our God is a consuming fire.*"[660]

APPLICATION IN OUR LIVES

Purpose in your heart to serve God. When you have opportunity, act. Do not let trivial or mortal fears prevent you from doing the work you are given to do. Teach the whole truth in love. Do not yield to the atheists, agnostics, pagans, or false teachers who would silence you.

Do not teach the gospel fearfully or apologetically, but with generosity of spirit, knowing that you are offering the greatest gift — the opportunity to find eternal life in Jesus Christ!

SEVEN-POINT DISCUSSION GUIDE

1. False Teaching: Some people teach that human suffering is proof that God is not a good God or that He does not exist. They imagine that railing against God is like dealing with human authorities by "speaking truth to power."

    Why is this human foolishness?

2. Why do we fear God?

3. Why do we love God?

4. Why can we trust God?

5. We are commanded not to fear man or even death. What happens against God's will when we do fear man or death?

6. What has the Lord done to make it possible for us not to fear death?

7. Encouraging the younger preacher, Timothy, to remain faithful despite his suffering for the gospel, Paul wrote, "For God has not given us a spirit of fear, but of power and of love and of a sound mind" (2 Timothy 1:7). Contrast fear to these three gifts of God, telling how fear is different.

FEAR	GOD'S GIFTS
	Power
	Love
	A Sound Mind

CALL TO ACTION

Listen to your own thinking for the next week.

Do you hear yourself saying or thinking, "I am afraid"?

Make notes of the things you are allowing yourself to worry about.

Pray to God about them and notice how few, if any, of the things you feared came to pass.

SONG AND PSALM

LIVING BY FAITH

PSALMS 27; A PSALM OF DAVID.
The Lord is my light and my salvation;
    Whom shall I fear?
    The Lord is the strength of my life;
    Of whom shall I be afraid?
When the wicked came against me
    To eat up my flesh,
    My enemies and foes,
    They stumbled and fell.
Though an army may encamp against me,
    My heart shall not fear;
    Though war may rise against me,
    In this I will be confident.

One thing I have desired of the Lord,
    That will I seek:
    That I may dwell in the house of the Lord
    All the days of my life,
    To behold the beauty of the Lord,
    And to inquire in His temple.

For in the time of trouble
 He shall hide me in His pavilion;
 In the secret place of His tabernacle
 He shall hide me;
 He shall set me high upon a rock.

And now my head shall be lifted up above my enemies all around me;
 Therefore I will offer sacrifices of joy in His tabernacle;
 I will sing, yes, I will sing praises to the LORD.

Hear, O LORD, when I cry with my voice!
 Have mercy also upon me, and answer me.
When You said, "Seek My face,"
 My heart said to You, "Your face, LORD, I will seek."
Do not hide Your face from me;
 Do not turn Your servant away in anger;
 You have been my help;
 Do not leave me nor forsake me,
 O God of my salvation.
When my father and my mother forsake me,
 Then the LORD will take care of me.

Teach me Your way, O LORD,
 And lead me in a smooth path, because of my enemies.
Do not deliver me to the will of my adversaries;
 For false witnesses have risen against me,
 And such as breathe out violence.
I would have lost heart, unless I had believed
 That I would see the goodness of the LORD
 In the land of the living.

Wait on the LORD;
 Be of good courage,
 And He shall strengthen your heart;
 Wait, I say, on the LORD![661]

BE KEEPERS

SUGGESTED TOPIC FOR PRAYER

Pray for your faith to be founded in the love of God, confidence in the salvation of Jesus' Christ, and for a sound mind to understand the will of God in times of trial.

LESSON 13

BE FOUND WATCHFUL

*"Take heed, watch and pray; for you do not know when the time is.
... And what I say to you, I say to all: Watch!"*

Mark 13:33, 37

Jesus calls us to prayerful vigilance. He commands us to "Watch!" Watching is active anticipation of His return. He commands us individually and collectively to be on watch; ever wary, ever expecting, ever prepared, and ever prayerful! We anticipate the return of the Lord, God's great and terrible day of judgment, the end of this world, and the dawn of an eternal day of the kingdom of God in heaven.

BEE-ATTITUDE: WATCHFULNESS

Every part of a honeybee's half inch long body is purposefully designed. The bee's antennae and five eyes allow the insect to be extremely vigilant. The antennae feel/hear vibrations and smell with 170 odor receptors. A bee's two large compound eyes use 6,900 lenses to produce a mosaic image that is assembled in the bee's brain even when flying at 15 miles per hour. Tiny hairs between the components of the eyes determine wind direction. The three small eyes on the top of a honeybee's head perceive ultraviolet light even through dense cloud cover. These eyes allow honeybees to triangulate their location as they travel between flowers and the hive. Bees can see ultraviolet patches on flowers that are invisible to human eyes but guide the insects to find nectar and ensure the plant's pollination. Bees are designed to be watchful for danger, food sources, and the way home. Christian women are also to be watchful. The psalmist praised God saying, *"The eyes of all look expectantly to You, and You give them their food in due season. You open Your hand and satisfy the desire of every living thing."*[662]

Like the Creator's honeybees, we vigilantly watch for sin's danger, seek spiritual nourishment from God's Word and His church, and look toward our eternal home. Watching helps us remain faithful to the end, whether it is until our own death or until Christ's return.

The compelling verses quoted above are from Jesus' description of the end of this world. He commanded us to listen, watch, and pray for His return. Other Scriptures teach us to watch for spiritual dangers, false teachers, and one another's souls, as well as our Lord's return. In Luke 18:8, Jesus shared a parable that encouraged Christians to persist in prayer for justice. He closed with an ominous question, *"Nevertheless, when the Son of Man comes, will He really find faith on the earth?"* If we are here at His return, don't we hope to greet Jesus Christ as the faithful? John closed the book of Revelation with Jesus' words, *"Surely I am coming quickly."* In the fullness of his faith, John was able to add, *"Amen. Even so, come, Lord Jesus!"*[663] Are you ready to pray that prayer?

BE WATCHFUL

Mark 13:32-37

"But of that day and hour no one knows, not even the angels in heaven, nor the Son, but only the Father.

Take heed, watch and pray; for you do not know when the time is.

It is like a man going to a far country, who left his house and gave authority to his servants, and to each his work, and commanded the doorkeeper to watch.

Watch therefore, for you do not know when the master of the house is coming—in the evening, at midnight, at the crowing of the rooster, or in the morning—lest, coming suddenly, he find you sleeping.

And what I say to you, I say to all: Watch!"[664]

YOUR WATCH STATIONS

The Old Testament book of Nehemiah was written while Nehemiah served as the cupbearer to King Artaxerxes during the latter part of Judah's Babylonian captivity. By the providence of God, the pagan king allowed and equipped Nehemiah to return to Judah to rebuild the walls of Jerusalem. The work progressed quickly, *"for the people had a mind to work."*[665]

Their adversaries decided that killing the workers was the only thing that would cause the work to cease. Nehemiah then set a watch and assigned people to work on sections of the wall near their families. He positioned half the people to work on the construction while the other half stood watch. Those who worked also held weapons. Those who watched were dressed in armor and equipped with spears, shields, and bows! They slept in their clothes to be ready to fight if attacked by night. The wall was finished in just 52 days, and all *"perceived that this work was done by our God."*[666]

AT YOUR OWN HOUSE

Nehemiah's work to restore Jerusalem did not end there, nor did the need to be watchful. After the last gate was hung, he directed, *"Do not let the gates of Jerusalem be opened until the sun is hot; and while they stand guard, let them shut and bar the doors; and appoint guards from among the inhabitants of Jerusalem, one at his watch station and another in front of his own house."*[667] Being watchful means never letting our guard down and barring the enemy from our lives day and night. It begins at our own house!

Do you guard the entrance to your home? The devil brings sin under your roof through the television, internet, newspapers, streaming services, cell phones, fashion industry, popular books, and worldly friends who work to lower your dedication to God. When I was about 14, my father made me break a 45 rpm record I had bought because the song used the word *hell* as a curse word. I was embarrassed but impressed that Dad didn't just want it out of our house. He would not have allowed me to give it to someone at school. Dad wanted it destroyed.

My husband and I turn off many movies over offensive language, immoral activities, immodest dress, adultery, homosexuality, and violence. You are right; that is most programming. Our grown children limit the grandchildren's screen time and screen the programs they see. Cartoons are not automatically safe fare for children. The animated film industry has an increasingly ungodly, progressive agenda. Even when it is not overtly making people laugh at sin, it is laying down premises that will serve their godless propaganda. Many Christian families are choosing private schools or homeschooling because the public schools are being used to promote atheism, evolution, socialism, world religions, abortion, feminism, homosexuality, sex changes, underage sexual activity, and are often doing so without parental knowledge or consent. Even elementary school counseling curricula are designed to sever children from their families' values, calling them outdated traditions.

IN GOD'S HOUSE

Nehemiah also brought God's Word before the people of Jerusalem. Chapter eight begins, *"Now all the people gathered together as one man in the open square that was in front of the Water Gate; and they told Ezra the scribe to bring the Book of the Law of Moses, which the Lord had commanded Israel. So Ezra the priest brought the Law before the assembly of menmen and women and all who could hear with understanding on the first day of the seventh month. Then he read from it in the open square that was in front of the Water Gate from morning until midday, before the men and women and those who could understand; and the ears of all the people were attentive to the Book of the Law."*[668]

Being watchful requires that our families are knowledgeable of the Bible. Not only did the people stand to hear the Word of God read in Jerusalem, but they also responded with great remorse. Ezra prayed, praised God, and read from the Law of Moses. *"Then all the people answered, "Amen, Amen!" while lifting up their hands. And they bowed their heads and worshiped the Lord with their faces to the ground."*[669] Nehemiah said, *"all the people wept, when they heard the words of the Law."* God turned their mourning to rejoicing. They were told, *"This day is holy to the Lord your God; do not mourn nor weep... Go your way, eat the fat, drink the sweet, and send portions to those for whom nothing is prepared; for this day is holy to our Lord. Do not sorrow, for the joy of the Lord is your strength."*[670]

While we mourn the condition of the world around us, we keep watch over something even more precious than Jerusalem. We have been given His blood-bought church to steward and the good news of salvation in Jesus to proclaim! The Apostle Paul wrote, *"Therefore watch, and remember that for three years I did not cease to warn everyone (v.29: about false teachers) night and day with tears."*[671] We rejoice in the hope of glory, of eternal life restored to the presence of God.

Christians have many great reasons to rejoice! We rejoice with heaven when a sinner comes to Christ. We rejoice when a brother or sister is restored. We take great joy in worshipping God with His people. We celebrate the translation and distribution of God's Word to many nations and the courageous missionary families in the fields. We share communion each week in memory of Christ and His sacrifice for our sin, as do our brethren all around the globe on the first day of every week.

IN OUR DAILY LIVES

The remainder of the book of Nehemiah and the book of Ezra record the work of getting the lives of Judah right with God and with their neighbors. All their enemies were not outside the city wall. They had to end sins of financial usury, enslavement of their brethren, and marriages that violated God's law. The leaders exacted oaths and ensured that what the men promised was done. The practices of worship and priestly sacrifice had to be restored. Everything pagan was removed. Soon the city of Jerusalem was filled with songs of praise and rejoicing. Removing sin from our lives, committing to worshipping God in Spirit and Truth, and watching for His return will also give us cause to rejoice!

KEEPING WATCH

"Now there were in the same country shepherds living out in the fields, keeping watch over their flock by night. And behold, an angel of the Lord stood

before them, and the glory of the Lord shone around them, and they were greatly afraid. Then the angel said to them, "Do not be afraid, for behold, I bring you good tidings of great joy which will be to all people. For there is born to you this day in the city of David a Savior, who is Christ the Lord."[672]

There is no more beautiful and poignant biblical metaphor than that of the Shepherd and the Lamb. Jesus is both our Good Shepherd and the perfect, firstborn, Lamb of God. How encouraging it is to mankind that the announcement of the birth of Immanuel was to shepherds who were keeping the night watch over their flock! Their fear was turned into joy for the long-awaited Messiah had been born in Bethlehem, the City of David! God's plan to redeem us from sin was coming to fruition.

About 30 years later when Jesus, the sinless Lamb of God, was about to be offered on the cross, He took His followers with Him to the garden of Gethsemane. There He went apart from them to pray. *"Then He came to the disciples and found them sleeping, and said to Peter, "What! Could you not watch with Me one hour? Watch and pray, lest you enter into temptation. The spirit indeed is willing, but the flesh is weak."*[673]

Jesus knew He was about to be sacrificed. It was the reason He had come into the world. He knew He would be resurrected on the third day, but Jesus also knew His disciples would be scattered and that the devil was eager to snatch them away, especially Peter.[674] In this unparalleled hour of trial, Christ charged His disciples to *"Watch and pray!"*

PARABLES OF WATCHFUL SERVANTS

When Jesus Christ came to Israel, He found many of their religious leaders neglecting and mistreating their neighbors. He used parables to convict them of abusing the people God had entrusted to them.

Jesus used parables to teach us to be watchful. Like servants entrusted with an estate, our fate will depend on how we have conducted His affairs. Watching for Jesus' return is not passive. He wants us to be busy about the work He has given us to do. The way we treat and care for others is an important part of keeping watch. *"Who then is a faithful and wise servant, whom his master made ruler over his household, to give them food in due season? Blessed is that servant whom his master, when he comes, will find so doing. Assuredly, I say to you that he will make him ruler over all his goods. But if that evil servant says in his heart, 'My master is delaying his coming,' and begins to beat his fellow servants, and to eat and drink with the drunkards, the master of that servant will come on a day when he is not looking for him and at an hour that he is not aware of, and will cut him in two and appoint him his portion with the hypocrites. There shall be weeping and gnashing of teeth.*[675]

Jesus emphasized that we must always be watchful, *"Let your waist be girded and your lamps burning; and you yourselves be like men who wait for their master, when he will return from the wedding, that when he comes and knocks they may open to him immediately. Blessed are those servants whom the master, when he comes, will find watching. Assuredly, I say to you that he will gird himself and have them sit down to eat, and will come and serve them. And if he should come in the second watch, or come in the third watch, and find them so, blessed are those servants."*[676] The parable is followed with the clear, cautionary command, *"Therefore you also be ready, for the Son of Man is coming at an hour you do not expect."*[677]

There is no room for complacency nor time for sinful self-indulgence. All four Gospels record Jesus' saying He would return, and three emphasize that His return will be unexpected, *"But take heed to yourselves, lest your hearts be weighed down with carousing, drunkenness, and cares of this life, and that Day come on you unexpectedly. For it will come as a snare on all those who dwell on the face of the whole earth. Watch therefore, and pray always that you may be counted worthy to escape all these things that will come to pass, and to stand before the Son of Man."*[678]

Can you hear the strains of Fanny Crosby's hymn, "Will Jesus Find Us Watching?"

> *When Jesus comes to reward His servants,*
> *Whether it be noon or night,*
> *Faithful to Him will He find us watching,*
> *With our lamps all trimmed and bright?*
>
> *If, at the dawn of the early morning,*
> *He shall call us one by one,*

When to the Lord we restore our talents,
Will He answer you, "Well done?"

Blessed are those whom the Lord finds watching,
In His glory they shall share;
If He shall come at the dawn or midnight,
Will He find us watching there?

Refrain:
O can we say we are ready, brother?
Ready for the soul's bright home?
Say, will He find you and me still watching,
Waiting, watching when the Lord shall come?[679]

Jesus warned His followers to be ready for two events. The first was God's judgment against Israel when Jerusalem fell to the Romans and the temple was destroyed ending the Jews' ability to offer daily sacrifices, the Old Law had been fulfilled, nailed to the cross as all of

God's people were then and are now to hear Jesus Christ. This event came to pass in A.D. 70. The historian, Josephus, tells us that the warnings were so clear that no Christians were lost when Jerusalem was besieged. Being watchful as commanded by Jesus, the Christians had all fled to the hills.[680]

When we are watching, we are ready for the Lord's return. The second event that His disciples asked about was the end of the age. We watch and wait for it as did the churches of the first century. Paul's words of encouragement remain for us as long as the world stands, *"Watch, stand fast in the faith, be brave, be strong. Let all that you do be done with love.*[681] *Our task remains to be ready! "Therefore let us not sleep, as others do, but let us watch and be sober."*[682]

We fight a battle against ancient foes but with God on our side. They, like Goliath, stand no chance against our God. Yet we, like David, must have faith and be prepared to take our stand in the name of God. Read the familiar passage below, and note how we prepare to fight the good fight.

EPHESIANS 6:14-20

"Stand therefore, having girded your waist with truth, having put on the breastplate of righteousness, and having shod your feet with the preparation of the gospel of peace; above all, taking the shield of faith with which you will be able to quench all the fiery darts of the wicked one. And take the helmet of salvation, and the sword of the Spirit, which is the word of God; praying always with all prayer and supplication in the Spirit, being watchful to this end with all perseverance and supplication for all the saints- and for me (Paul), that utterance may be given to me, that I may open my mouth boldly to make known the mystery of the gospel, for which I am an ambassador in chains; that in it I may speak boldly, as I ought to speak."[683]

THEY WATCH FOR YOUR SOULS

We all have a responsibility to watch for one another, for our children and grandchildren, for our spouse, for our brothers and sisters in Christ, for our neighbors in every nation under heaven. Like Timothy, preachers have a responsibility to be watchful in all things and teach the truth soundly, knowing the church well enough to rebuke and exhort as needed. These are Paul's words to Timothy that the Holy Spirit has preserved for all who preach,

> "I charge you therefore before God and the Lord Jesus Christ, who will judge the living and the dead at His appearing and His kingdom: Preach the word! Be ready in season and out of season. Convince, rebuke, exhort, with all longsuffering and teaching. For the time will come when they will not endure sound doctrine, but according to their own desires, because they have itching ears, they will heap up for themselves teachers; and they will turn their ears away from the

truth, and be turned aside to fables. But you be watchful in all things, endure afflictions, do the work of an evangelist, fulfill your ministry."[684]

The elders of a congregation have been given an injunction to watch for our souls. The apostle John modeled that role in the New Testament, writing to the churches, *"I have no greater joy than to hear that my children walk in truth."*[685] Paul called the elders from Ephesus overseers when he sent for them to meet him at a seaport to deliver this message,

"For I have not shunned to declare to you the whole counsel of God. Therefore take heed to yourselves and to all the flock, among which the Holy Spirit has made you overseers, to shepherd the church of God which He purchased with His own blood. For I know this, that after my departure savage wolves will come in among you, not sparing the flock. Also from among yourselves men will rise up, speaking perverse things, to draw away the disciples after themselves. Therefore watch, and remember that for three years I did not cease to warn everyone night and day with tears. So now, brethren, I commend you to God and to the word of His grace, which is able to build you up and give you an inheritance among all those who are sanctified" (Acts 20:37-32).

Our responsibility is to submit to the leadership of the elders. *"Obey those who rule over you, and be submissive, for they watch out for your souls, as those who must give account. Let them do so with joy and not with grief, for that would be unprofitable for you."*[686]

WATCH FOR HIS RETURN

Jesus left His disciples with the wonderful promises of His return. *"In My Father's house are many mansions; if it were not so, I would have told you. I go to prepare a place for you. And if I go and prepare a place for you, I will come again and receive you to Myself; that where I am, there you may be also."*[687] Daniel prophesied of that day,

"At that time Michael shall stand up,
The great prince who stands watch over the sons of your people;
And there shall be a time of trouble,

Such as never was since there was a nation,
Even to that time.
And at that time your people shall be delivered,
Every one who is found written in the book.
And many of those who sleep in the dust of the earth shall awake,
Some to everlasting life,
Some to shame and everlasting contempt.
Those who are wise shall shine
Like the brightness of the firmament,
And those who turn many to righteousness
Like the stars forever and ever."[688]

Our Lord also left His Apostles and disciples with the commendation, *"Watch therefore, for you do not know what hour your Lord is coming."*[689] *"Take heed, watch and pray; for you do not know when the time is."*[690] His warning is for all people in all places at all times, *"And what I say to you, I say to all: Watch!"*[691]

The writer of Hebrews emphasized the danger of rebelliously choosing to live in sin after having known the truth, *"For if we sin willfully after we have received the knowledge of the truth, there no longer remains a sacrifice for sins, but a certain fearful expectation of judgment, and fiery indignation which will devour the adversaries. Anyone who has rejected Moses' law dies without mercy on the testimony of two or three witnesses. Of how much worse punishment, do you suppose, will he be thought worthy who has trampled the Son of God underfoot, counted the blood of the covenant by which he was sanctified a common thing, and insulted the Spirit of grace?"*[692]

The New Testament ends with letters from the apostles, Peter and John; the Lord's brothers, James and Jude; and the Revelation given by the ascended Lord to the apostle John. Their words echo Jesus' words and remind us of the importance of remaining watchful and testify of their confidence in Jesus' promises.

> "But the end of all things is at hand; therefore be serious and watchful in your prayers. And above all things have fervent love for one another, for "love will cover a multitude of sins." Be hospitable to one

another without grumbling. As each one has received a gift, minister it to one another, as good stewards of the manifold grace of God."[693]

"Therefore be patient, brothers, until the coming of the Lord. Behold, the farmer waits for the precious fruit of the soil, being patient concerning it until it receives the early and late rains. You also be patient. Strengthen your hearts, because the coming of the Lord is near."[694]

"But you, beloved, building yourselves up on your most holy faith, praying in the Holy Spirit, keep yourselves in the love of God, looking for the mercy of our Lord Jesus Christ unto eternal life."[695]

"Remember therefore how you have received and heard; hold fast and repent. Therefore if you will not watch, I will come upon you as a thief, and you will not know what hour I will come upon you."[696]

TRUST IN HIS PROMISES

Still, Christians need not dread the final judgment! The New Testament is filled with assurances so that we may look longingly toward seeing Him face to face. Paul wrote, "For now we see in a mirror, dimly, but then face to face. Now I know in part, but then I shall know just as I also am known."[697] Despite being called by Christ while on the road to persecute Christians in Damascus, Paul was confident that, through Jesus, he had been forgiven, writing, *"For I am persuaded that neither death nor life, nor angels nor principalities nor powers, nor things present nor things to come, nor height nor depth, nor any other created thing, shall be able to separate us from the love of God which is in Christ Jesus our Lord."*[698]

Titus 2:3 teaches that the older women should be reverent in behavior and teachers of good things. Christian women show reverence for God and His word through faith and good works. His promises are to everyone who is obedient to Christ; male or female, Jew or Gentile, slave or free.[699] We are to bless those who persecute us.[700] Live peaceably as much as depends on us.[701] Be ready to teach the truth in love when anyone asks about our faith.[702] Turn to God for help, praying without ceasing.[703] Endure, remaining faithful to the end, for the reward is beyond our ability to fathom. The hardships we endure in this life will be washed away in the endless day of eternity. God will not forsake us.

If we are focused on such spiritual things, we are being watchful. Jesus assures us of His abiding presence and advocacy, that God hears our prayers, and that our physical needs will be met in this life. Trusting God and building our lives on that hope frees us from the cares of this life to do the work God sends us to do. Releasing temporal things (e.g. possessions, pride, fear), we are strengthened against temptation and made able to love one another as Christ loves us.

Confidence is a part of faith, perhaps a synonym for the sure hope we have in God's promises. We are made confident of His promises because our God is holy, loving, and does not/cannot lie.[704] Examine promises God and Jesus have made to the church. These scriptures strengthen our faith and give us confidence in our salvation. In the scriptures below, we will examine many of God's promises, grouped as *Promises of His Care*, *Promises of Salvation*, *Promises of God's Faithfulness*, *Promises for Tribulation*, and *Promises of Eternal Life in Heaven*. May your soul be edified, and your faith be strengthened for God's glory. As you read each passage, take time to reflect on how it affects your faith and/or motivates your good works of obedience.

PROMISES OF HIS CARE

Underline the promise(s) in each passage.

"But seek first the kingdom of God and His righteousness, and all these things (v 31-32 food, water, clothing) shall be added to you."[705]

"And I tell you, ask and it will be given to you; seek and you will find; knock and it will be opened for you. For everyone who asks receives, and the one who seeks finds, and to the one who knocks it will be opened."[706]

"And Jesus came and spoke to them, saying, "All authority has been given to Me in heaven and on earth. Go therefore and

For example: I can focus on things of God in this lifetime because He will take care of my physical needs.

make disciples of all the nations, baptizing them in the name of the Father and of the Son and of the Holy Spirit, teaching them to observe all things that I have commanded you; and lo, I am with you always, *even* to the end of the age. Amen."[707]

PROMISES OF SALVATION

Salvation is both escaping condemnation and attaining eternal life with our God. Some people worry that fear of hell is an inadequate motivation for becoming a Christian, but that great day of the Lord's return will be a terrible day of condemnation and judgment for many, many souls. Sermons that warn of hell are few, but this should not be so. We are to fear God as well as love Him. We teach others because we are sent to do so. Understanding one's lost[704] Titus 1:2 as variously translated: (NKJV), "in hope of eternal life which God, **who cannot lie**, promised before time began"; (ESV) "in hope of eternal life, which God, **who never lies**, promised before the ages began"; (YLT) "upon hope of life age-during, which God, **who doth not lie**, did promise before times of ages."

PROMISES OF SALVATION

Underline the promise(s) in each passage.

- "He who believes and is baptized will be saved; but he who does not believe will be condemned."[708]

- "In this the love of God was manifested toward us, that God has sent His only begotten Son into the world, that we might live through Him."[709]

- "Jesus said to her, "I am the resurrection and the life. He who believes in Me, though he may die, he shall live. And whoever lives and believes in Me shall never die. Do you believe this?"[710]

"Then the King will say to those on His right hand, 'Come, you blessed of My Father, inherit the kingdom prepared for you from the foundation of the world.'"[711]

PROMISES OF GOD'S FAITHFULNESS

In today's world, we see the evils of hatred and violence that motivated God to destroy the world with the great flood. We see the idolatry and lack of faith that made God destroy many Israelites in the wilderness. We see the sins that brought destruction on Sodom and Gomorrah. We see men and women who seek to mislead God's people for their own gain, sins that caused the destruction of Jerusalem. Do you wonder if God's wrath might come against our generation? Allow God's faithfulness to secure your joy in salvation.

PROMISES OF GOD'S FAITHFULNESS

Underline the promise(s) in each passage.

"God is not a man, that He should lie,
Nor a son of man, that He should repent.
Has He said, and will He not do?
Or has He spoken, and will He not make it good?"[712]

"*Through* the LORD's mercies we are not consumed,
Because His compassions fail not.
They are new every morning;
Great *is* Your faithfulness.
"The LORD *is* my portion," says my soul,
"Therefore I hope in Him!"[713]

"But the Lord is faithful,
who will establish you and guard *you* from the evil one."[714]

"Let us hold fast the confession of our hope without wavering,
for He who promised is faithful."[715]

"God *is* faithful, by whom you were called into the fellowship
of His Son, Jesus Christ our Lord."[716]

"If we confess our sins, He is faithful and just to forgive us *our* sins and to cleanse us from all unrighteousness."[717]

"Forever, O LORD, Your word is settled in heaven.
Your faithfulness *endures* to all generations."[718]

JOSEPH'S EXAMPLE OF GOD'S FAITHFUL PROVIDENCE

When evildoers seem to flourish, it helps to remember that God is ultimately in control. Continue to live righteously. Watch for His hand in your life. This is providence. The stories of Joseph's life and trials inspire trust in God's providence for many Christians. Joseph was only 17 years old when his envious brothers sold him into slavery and convinced his father that he was killed by a wild beast. Joseph's faith in God made it possible for him to see God's providence at work through 13 years of slavery and unjust imprisonment. Joseph's faith was manifested in his godly character. God blessed his work in Potiphar's household and again in the prison until his masters knew nothing of their own affairs but entrusted everything to Joseph because they could see God blessing him.[719]

Joseph did not become conceited in times of prosperity, nor charge God when he was unjustly accused by Potiphar's wife and imprisoned. He did not lose hope when Pharaoh's butler forgot about him in prison for two more years. Nor did Joseph become corrupted with power when he rose to prominence in Egypt at the age of 30. When he came face to face with the brothers who betrayed him, Joseph was able to see how his circumstances had been used by God to bring about the preservation of the family God had chosen to be His people.[720] As his brothers bowed before him, Joseph said, *"Do not be afraid, for am I in the place of God? But as for you, you meant evil against me; but God meant it for good, in order to bring it about as it is this day, to save many people alive. Now therefore, do not be afraid; I will provide for you and your little ones."* And he *comforted them and spoke kindly to them.*"[721] What a wonderful example of forgiveness, of faith to trust God, and not lean on our own understanding!

Miracles of God that altered the normal progression of things were not commonplace, even in Old Testament times, but those that He wrought were recorded in the scriptures to build faith and prepare mankind for the fulfillment of God's glorious, merciful plan for our redemption. Miracles of the New Testament served to confirm Jesus' deity and God's Word until the New Testament Scriptures were complete. In addition to the overtly miraculous acts of God, He has c used the natural world and the things people, kings, and nations do to accomplish His purposes throughout time. This has been described as God's providence.[722]

Stephen's sermon recounted the history of God's people to convict his Jewish audience of their sin in rejecting Christ. Stephen spoke of Joseph's brothers, saying, *"And the patriarchs, becoming envious, sold Joseph into Egypt. But God was with him."*[723] Recall the dream of Joseph in which his brothers were represented as sheaves of wheat bowing to Joseph's sheaf. Because their hearts were blinded by hatred, they saw a prophecy of having to submit to their younger brother. They did not respect that this dream was from God. They were willing to kill him or sell him into slavery to keep the inheritance they imagined would be taken from them. The brothers were willing to break their father's heart to avoid the dream's fulfillment. Unlike Joseph, they were willing to sin against God.

Joseph's second dream was of the sun, moon, and 11 stars bowing to him. If his brothers were able to think past their envy, this dream ruled out their misinterpretation that Joseph would take their birthright. How different the brothers' attitude would have been toward Joseph if they had realized the dreams foretold that he would be their families' lifeline in a seven-year-long famine!

On the day of Pentecost, Jews who heard Peter's sermon were cut to the heart and responded by asking what to do. They confessed belief in Christ, repented, and were baptized for the remission of their sins. God added them to His church. The Jewish leaders who heard Stephen's sermon were also 'cut to the heart' but responded in anger. *"Then they cried out with a loud voice, stopped their ears, and ran at him with one accord; and they cast him out of the city and stoned him.*[724]

Joseph's brothers and their families received deliverance by God's providence despite their sin and were able to repent and reconcile with Joseph. The Jews who stoned Stephen had rejected Christ. How differently they might have responded to Stephen if their hearts been truly watching for the Salvation of Israel!

Today, we face the same dilemma. We can be gullible to the devil's deceptions and cling to things of this world, condemning our own souls, or we can submit to God's will and know untold glories await us eternally.

PROMISES FOR TRIBULATION

Our brothers and sisters in India worship God among the pagan temples of their Hindu neighbors, some of whom have grown increasingly hostile toward Christianity. In Muslim and communist nations, our brethren risk persecution and execution for their faith. In our own nation, atheists and other non-Christians mock His name and openly seek to silence God's Word and use media, government, the courts, and schools to promote evil and falsely accuse His saints.

What is our response to be? Love. Love one another, including those who choose to act as our enemies.[725] Live peaceably as much as depends on us.[726] Be ready to teach the truth in love if anyone asks about our faith.[727] Turn to God for help.[728] Pray without ceasing.[729] Endure, remain faithful to the end, for the reward is great.[730] The hardships we endure in this life will be insignificant in eternity.[731] God will not forsake us even if the trials come to bloodshed.[732]

PROMISES FOR TRIBULATION

Underline the promise(s) in each passage.

"Be strong and of good courage, do not fear nor be afraid of them; for the LORD your God, He *is* the One who goes with you. He will not leave you nor forsake you."[733]

"For God has not given us a spirit of fear, but of power and of love and of a sound mind."[734]

"Do not fear any of those things which you are about to suffer. Indeed, the devil is about to throw *some* of you into prison, that you may be tested, and you will have tribulation ten days. Be faithful until death, and I will give you the crown of life."[735]

"Because you have kept My command to persevere, I also will keep you from the hour of trial which shall come upon the whole world, to test those who dwell on the earth."[736]

PROMISES OF ETERNAL LIFE

Here we are pilgrims, sojourners in our land of Egypt. We are sanctified by God's Word of Truth, set apart to do God's will. We remain in this world to be a light for the nations. Our Lord and King, Jesus Christ submitted to death on the cross. His only explanation to Pilate was, *"My kingdom is not of this world. If My kingdom were of this world, My servants would fight, so that I should not be delivered to the Jews; but now My kingdom is not from here."*[737] He prayed for us before His death that while we remain in this world, God would keep us from the evil one.[738] He promised to return for us. Peter wrote that we *"look for new heavens and a new earth in which righteousness dwells."*[739] This world is not our home, *"For here we have no continuing city, but we seek the one to come."*[740] We do not try to accumulate wealth here but invest in the care of our neighbors, laying up treasure in heaven. We know only a little of the spiritual realm, but Jesus came down from above and ascended to rule at God's right hand. Therefore, we can be confident in His promises of that eternal home of the soul!

PROMISES OF ETERNAL LIFE IN HEAVEN

Underline the promise(s) in each passage.

"Let not your heart be troubled; you believe in God, believe also in Me. In My Father's house are many mansions; if *it were* not *so*, I would have told you. I go to prepare a place for you. And if I go and prepare a place for you, I will come again and receive you to Myself; that where I am, *there* you may be also."[741]

"But when the kindness and the love of God our Savior toward man appeared, not by works of righteousness which we have done, but according to His mercy He saved us, through the washing of regeneration and renewing of the Holy Spirit, whom He poured out on us abundantly through Jesus Christ our Savior, that having been justified by His grace we should become heirs according to the hope of eternal life."[742]

"He who overcomes shall be clothed in white garments, and I will not blot out his name from the Book of Life; but I will confess his name before My Father and before His angels."[743]

APPLICATION IN OUR LIVES

- Do attend worship and Bible study in person every time the church gathers, but don't stop there.
- Worship to please God, not yourself. Study God's Word, but don't stop there.
- Do what His scriptures teach. Meet to the needs of your family, fellow Christians, and neighbors, but don't stop there.
- Watch for sin in your own life. Guard against false teachings and worldly doctrines that endanger souls, but don't stop there.
- Warn others. Teach the gospel. Pray without ceasing, but don't stop there.
- Repent with godly sorrow when you sin. Let go of this world and live for eternity. There is no place to stop until our Lord Jesus Christ returns.

Is something in the way of your being able to pray, *"Come quickly, Lord Jesus"*? If it is sin, remove it from your life. If it is the unsaved condition of the souls of those you love, then pray, set a godly example, and teach the truth if they will hear you. Send another teacher if you are not the right messenger. If you love this world, beware. We are so blessed! Our family time is precious. Sometimes leaving the known for the unknown is difficult, but the eternal home prepared for us is beyond our ability to imagine. Our God is good.

> *"Eye has not seen, nor ear heard,*
> *Nor have entered into the heart of man*
> *The things which God has prepared for those who love Him."*[744]

Joseph endured 13 years of hardship among the pagans of Egypt. The dreams he had been given and God's abiding presence gave Joseph hope. God's promises to His church are our source of hope. We can be confident in that hope. According to Hebrews, God has built the house. Moses was a faithful servant there, *"but Christ (is) a Son over His own house, whose house we are if we hold fast the confidence and the rejoicing of the hope firm to the end."*[745] There is a place prepared for you and me. Remain watchful.

SEVEN-POINT DISCUSSION GUIDE

1. False Teaching: Some people teach that it is impossible to understand God's Word and discern how He wants us to worship, live, and serve Him. How would you refute this?

2. What does Jesus mean when He commands us to pray and watch? Nehemiah had families rebuild the wall and stand guard near their own homes. What was the impact?

3. How do Christian women, men, preachers, and elders watch for others' souls?

4. Why do we both love and fear God? Why aren't these commands contradictory?

5. Describe the reasons Christians can come confidently before God's throne in prayer? Describe the reasons Christians can come before His throne at judgment?

6. As you studied the promises of God featured in this lesson, what did you notice that strengthens your faith?

7. When someone asks you the reason for the hope that is in you, how will you explain your confidence in God's redemption through Jesus Christ? (See guidance under Suggested Topic for Prayer, below.)

SONG OR PSALM

"WHEN THE ROLL IS CALLED UP YONDER"
"ON CHRIST THE SOLID ROCK I STAND"

PSALM 145: A PRAISE PSALM OF DAVID
I will extol You, my God, O King;
And I will bless Your name forever and ever.
Every day I will bless You,
And I will praise Your name forever and ever.
Great is the LORD, and greatly to be praised;
And His greatness is unsearchable.
One generation shall praise Your works to another,

And shall declare Your mighty acts.
I will meditate on the glorious splendor of Your majesty,
And on Your wondrous works.
Men shall speak of the might of Your awesome acts,
And I will declare Your greatness.
They shall utter the memory of Your great goodness,
And shall sing of Your righteousness.
The Lord is gracious and full of compassion,
Slow to anger and great in mercy.
The Lord is good to all,
And His tender mercies are over all His works.
All Your works shall praise You, O Lord,
And Your saints shall bless You.
They shall speak of the glory of Your kingdom,
And talk of Your power,
To make known to the sons of men His mighty acts,
And the glorious majesty of His kingdom.
Your kingdom is an everlasting kingdom,
And Your dominion endures throughout all generations.
The Lord upholds all who fall,
And raises up all who are bowed down.
The eyes of all look expectantly to You,
And You give them their food in due season.
You open Your hand
And satisfy the desire of every living thing.
The Lord is righteous in all His ways,
Gracious in all His works.
The Lord is near to all who call upon Him,
To all who call upon Him in truth.
He will fulfill the desire of those who fear Him;
He also will hear their cry and save them.
The Lord preserves all who love Him,
But all the wicked He will destroy.
My mouth shall speak the praise of the Lord,
And all flesh shall bless His holy name
Forever and ever.[746]

BE KEEPERS

SUGGESTED TOPIC FOR PRAYER

Pray for wisdom and courage to watch vigilantly and wait expectantly upon the Lord.

Pray as Nehemiah did before he made important decisions, then take time to write out your reason for the hope that is in you. Share it with another sister in Christ. Watch and pray for opportunities to share the gospel with those outside of Christ and do the good works that we are called to do to His glory.

EPILOGUE

BE LOVERS OF GOD'S WORD

"All flesh is as grass,
And all the glory of man as the flower of the grass.
The grass withers,
And its flower falls away,
But the word of the Lord endures forever."

1 Peter 1:24-25

Precious Sisters,

We must be lovers of God's Word who are delighted to obey His commandments. Studying Scripture cannot be an academic exercise because it is the living Word of God. The moment it enters the ear, it begins to work on the heart. Receptive hearts will open, but hearts that reject the gospel will harden to resist its blade. *"For the word of God is living and powerful, and sharper than any two-edged sword, piercing even to the division of soul and spirit, and of joints and marrow, and is a discerner of the thoughts and intents of the heart."*[747] If we welcome Truth, we will not mind when His Word severs us from sin and worldliness nor hesitate when it calls us to act in service to others.

False teachers only live one lifetime, but lies originate from the devil who deceives every generation. A day is coming when deceit will end. When Christ returns, those Christians who lived obedient to the gospel will be saved by His grace. Those who refused the Son of God will face eternal torment. In the light of His presence, only Truth will remain.

God's Word is our hope. His grace is our salvation. You may be a young woman anticipating decades in God's service or a mature sister in Christ teaching and encouraging others. Wherever you are, love those around you without self-concerns. Obey without fear. Be a student of God's Word and act on it in every way. Pray continually.

Peter closed his second epistle with these words that I humbly borrow for your edification, *"Grow in the grace and knowledge of our Lord and Savior Jesus Christ. To Him be the glory both now and forever. Amen"* (2 Peter 3:18).

Your sister in Jesus Christ,

Lisa

APPENDIX

HOW-TO LESSON FOR ANNOTATING TEXT

When reading Scripture and other texts, make notes to increase your focus and understanding. Put a symbol in the text you find significant and then write notes in a margin of your Bible or lesson book. Try using the four annotation symbols described below and shown in the example of verses on mercy from Chapter 1. Annotate any part of this book but certainly make notes about your thinking in the tables that provide a column for notes beside key Scriptures.

Use a + as a symbol for CONNECTIONS you make as you read.
Bible study is enriched by <u>connecting one passage to another</u>. This can be quoting what Jesus said about the topic, examining preceding or subsequent verses that provide context, noting other Scriptures on the same topic, and citing biblical examples or non-examples.

- Note another verse(s), write what Scripture says to confirm or extend the idea.
- Note parables or accounts from Scripture that teach about the topic.
- Note fulfillment of prophecy or witnesses of Jesus' deity.
- Note any apparent conflicts and study further to resolve them. (There are no actual contradictions in the Bible, but verses lifted

from context sometimes seem to disagree. Seek more information in a sound commentary or from a faithful Christian.)

You may also connect a Scripture <u>to your life</u> or <u>the world (society)</u>.

- Note how the passage shows right from wrong.
- Note how it affects your decision-making or shows you a need for repentance.
- Note how man-made doctrines or society's standards conflict with God's truth.

Use a ? as a symbol when QUESTIONS come to mind.

When you write out a question, you capture your thinking for careful consideration. This can lead to a deeper study on the topic or help you identify and clarify any misconception. To address your questions:

- Read verses before and after a verse to put it in context.
- Look up a key word in a concordance to find other Scriptures on the subject.
- Look at cross-references for the passage that are noted in your Bible.
- Refer to a sound Bible commentary on the passage.
- Ask a mature Christian, sharing the passage and your question.

Use a ★ for IMPORTANT STATEMENTS you want to remember or relocate.

Put a star by an important statement to help you locate it later. You may choose a criteria for a study and star occurrences. Examples: (1) Study Jesus' teachings in the gospels and place stars by His commands, promises, rebukes or commendations. (2) Study Acts or an epistle and star foundational truths, direct commands, practices in the early church, or passages from which you can infer God's will.

How-To Lesson for Annotating Text

Use an ! for MOTIVATING or INTERESTING statements.

We never stop discovering more as we read God's Word. When you notice things that you are excited to learn or share, the exclamation mark helps capture your reaction to the text.

ANNOTATION EXAMPLE

Scriptures about Showing Mercy

Matthew 5:7
"Blessed are the merciful,
For they shall obtain mercy."

'Jesus words. We must be merciful to receive His mercy = forgiveness of sin!

James 2:13
"For judgment is without mercy to the one who has shown no mercy. Mercy triumphs over judgment."

Connects to parable of unforgiving servant in Matt 18:21-35.
What does judgment mean here?

Mark 10:47
"And when he heard that it was Jesus of Nazareth, he began to cry out and say, "Jesus, Son of David, have mercy on me!"

Bartimaeus received sight, then followed Jesus on His triumphal entry into Jerusalem (c11). Wow!

REFERENCES

Coffman, James Burton. Coffman's Commentaries on the Bible, (1992). Retrieved from: https://www.studylight.org/commentaries/eng/bcc.html

Gospel Advocate New Testament Commentaries. Various authors. Gospel Advocate Publishers, Nashville, TN. Accessible online at https://www.restorationlibrary.org

Beepods, (2017). 10 Helpful Uses for Beeswax. https://www.beepods.com/10-helpful-uses- beeswax/

Beepods, (2017). 101 Fun BEE Facts About Bees and Beekeeping. https://www.beepods.com/101-fun-bee-facts-about-bees-and-beekeeping/

Blackiston, Howland. (2016). Understanding the role of the worker bee in a hive. https://www.dummies.com/article/home-auto-hobbies/hobby-farming/beekeeping/understanding-the-role-of-the-worker-bee-in-a-hive-188438

Bogdanov, Stefan. (2009). Beeswax Book. www.bee-hexagon.net British Library. Magna Carta (1216). https://www.bl.uk/onlinegallery/onlineex/histtexts/magna/index.html

Dorling-Kindersley (2016). Amazing Bees. DK Publishing, New York, New York.

Drug-like property profiling of novel neuroprotective compounds to treat acute ischemic stroke: guidelines to develop pleiotropic molecules. Lapchak PA. Transl Stroke Res. 2013 Jun;4(3):328-42. doi: 10.1007/s12975-012-0200-y. PMID: 23687519 Select item 14666245

Gelling, Natasha (2013). Smithsonian.com. The Science Behind Honey's Eternal Shelf Life. https://www.smithsonianmag.com/science-nature/the-science-behind-honeys-eternal-shelf- life-1218690/

Mandal, M. D., & Mandal, S. (2011). Honey: its medicinal property and antibacterial activity. Asian Pacific Journal of Tropical Biomedicine, 1(2), 154–160. http://doi.org/10.1016/S2221-1691(11)60016-6

Neuroprotection by flavonoids. Dajas F, Rivera-Megret F, Blasina F, Arredondo F, Abin- Carriquiry JA, Costa G, Echeverry C, Lafon L, Heizen H, Ferreira M, Morquio A. Braz J Med Biol Res. 2003 Dec;36(12):1613-20. Epub 2003 Nov 17. Review. PMID: 14666245

Oliver, Kyra. (2018). The power of beeswax lowers both pain and cholesterol. https://draxe.com/nutrition/beeswax/

Strong, James, (2009). Strong's Exhaustive Concordance. Tyndale House Publishers. Carol Stream, IL.

The Forest Charter (1225). https://www.bl.uk/collection-items/the-forest-charter-of-1225

The Natural Flavonoid Pinocembrin: Molecular Targets and Potential Therapeutic Applications. Lan X, Wang W, Li Q, Wang J. Mol Neurobiology. 2016 Apr;53(3):1794-1801. doi: 10.1007/s12035-015-9125-2. Epub 2015 Mar 7. Review.

Utah County Beekeepers Association. Fun Facts about Honeybees, Hives, and Honey. www.utahcountybeekeepers.com

Egyptian Hieroglyph of bee and honey jars, https://www.milkwood.net/2013/01/31/honeybee- democracy-the-sacred-bee-two-great-bee-books/

ENDNOTES

[1] Proverbs 30:24-28
[2] 1 John 5:2-3
[3] Matthew 22:34-40, John 15:9-17
[4] Matthew 25:31-40, Mark 16:15-16
[5] John 13:35
[6] Deuteronomy 6:5
[7] Leviticus 19:18
[8] Matthew 22:36-40
[9] Romans 14:7
[10] 1 Corinthians 12: 1-31, Titus 2:3-5
[11] Acts 10:34
[12] I Samuel 3:12-14
[13] I Samuel 4:18
[14] I Samuel 4:19-22
[15] 1 Samuel 1
[16] Deuteronomy 6:4-5
[17] 2 Peter 1:2-11
[18] Romans 13:8-10
[19] Romans 14: 10-13, quoting from Isaiah 45:23
[20] John 15:9-17
[21] Romans 14:15
[22] Philippians 2:3-4
[23] 1 Samuel 1, Numbers 30:6-8
[24] Matthew 22:39
[25] Matthew 5:38-48
[26] Romans 2:23, Matthew 18:21-35
[27] Luke 6:28
[28] Matthew 6:14-15, 18:35, Mark 11:25-26, Luke 23:34
[29] Hebrews 10:30, Jude 1
[30] Ephesians 4:31-32
[31] Colossians 1:18, 1 Thessalonians 1:1, Acts 20:28
[32] Luke 21:33, Matthew 16:8
[33] Mark 9:42-48, Luke 17:1-4
[34] Genesis 3:1-5
[35] James 1:17
[36] Titus 2:5
[37] Micah 6:8
[38] Matthew 5:16
[39] 1 Corinthians 11:1
[40] Philippians 3:9, Matthew 19:17
[41] Ephesians 1:13-14
[42] John 14:2-3
[43] Luke 18:18-19
[44] 1 Thessalonians 5:23
[45] John 15:12, 1 John 2:6, 3:3
[46] Luke 9:51-56
[47] 2 Kings 1
[48] Luke 9:55-56, John 3:16-17
[49] Hebrews 13:20-21
[50] Micah 6:8
[51] 1 Samuel 10—11
[52] 1 Samuel 11:13
[53] 1 Samuel 14:27-30
[54] 1 Samuel 14:43-45
[55] James 2:1-4, 2:8-9
[56] Deuteronomy 27:19
[57] Proverbs 21:3
[58] Proverbs 21:15
[59] Proverbs 28:5
[60] Zechariah 7:9
[61] Matthew 5:7
[62] James 2:13
[63] Mark 10:47
[64] Luke 10:36-37
[65] Ephesians 2:4-7
[66] 1 Corinthians 14:20
[67] James 3:17
[68] Luke 6:35-36
[69] 2 John 1:3
[70] Jeremiah 10:23
[71] Matthew 1:18-25
[72] 1 Peter 2:24
[73] 1 John 1:7
[74] Romans 12:14-21
[75] Titus 2
[76] Matthew 5:8
[77] Ephesians 6:9, Revelation 21:27

[78] Matthew 5:8, Luke 10:24
[79] Isaiah 33:17
[80] 1 John 1:1
[81] John 1:18
[82] John 1:14
[83] 1 John 3:1-3
[84] Isaiah 6:5
[85] Revelation 1:17
[86] 2 Corinthians 5:17-21, Romans 6:2-4, Revelation 1:5
[87] 1 John 3
[88] 1 John 1:9
[89] James 1:27, 3:17, 1 Peter 1:22, Revelation 20:12
[90] Hebrews 10:12-23
[91] Acts 15:8-9
[92] 1 Peter 1:22
[93] 1 Timothy 2:9-12, Deuteronomy 22:5
[94] 1 Peter 3:3-4, 1 Timothy 2:8-14
[95] Isaiah 53:2, John 12:32
[96] 2 Peter 2:9
[97] 1 Peter 3:1
[98] 1 Corinthians 6:8-10
[99] James 4:4, Ephesians 5:5, Revelation 2:4-5
[100] John 3:16-19, John 8:3-11
[101] Matthew 4:17, 5:48, Leviticus 11:45, 1 Peter 1:13
[102] Colossians 4:5-6
[103] Colossians 3:8-10
[104] Number 23:19, Titus 1:2, Hebrews 6:18, Proverbs 6:16-19
[105] John 17:17, Titus 1:2, Hebrews 6:18, John 8:44, Proverbs 6:16-19
[106] 1 Timothy 5:13, Psalm 1:1, Romans 14:17-19
[107] James 3:8-12, Ephesians 5:17-21
[108] Philippians 4:8-9
[109] Isaiah 63:8
[110] 2 Timothy 2:22
[111] 1 Thessalonians 4:1-8
[112] Hebrews 12:14-16
[113] 1 Thessalonians 4:1-8
[114] 1 Corinthians 6:9-20
[115] 1 John 3:3
[116] James 1:27
[117] Numbers 23:19, Galatians 6:7
[118] Psalm 18:26
[119] Leviticus 25:2-7
[120] Exodus 2:15
[121] John 1:29-36
[122] Matthew 15:7-9, quoting Isaiah 29:13, John 4:23-24, 1 John 3:3
[123] 1 Timothy 5:22
[124] 1 Peter 2:9-11, 2 Corinthians 6:17
[125] Hebrews 10:22
[126] Acts 20:7, I Corinthians 16:2
[127] 1 Peter 2:2
[128] James 1:22-25
[129] 1 Corinthians 11:27-29
[130] John 4:23-24
[131] 1 Timothy 1:5
[132] Philippians 3:3
[133] 1 Timothy 1:5
[134] 1 Timothy 5:21
[135] Ephesians 5:19, Colossians 3:16, Hebrew 2:12, Revelation 13:3
[136] Romans 8:26, 2 Corinthians 1:3, 2 Corinthians 13:9, Ephesians 6:18, Philippians 1:9, 1 Thessalonians 5:17, 5:25, James 5:16
[137] 1 Corinthians 9:5-7, Matthew 25, James 2:14-20
[138] 2 Samuel 11—12
[139] 2 Samuel 7:8-17, 7:27-29
[140] 1 Kings 12
[141] 2 Samuel 13—18
[142] 1 Kings 11:9-13
[143] 1 Kings 12
[144] 2 Chronicles 36:20-21, Daniel 9:1-2
[145] Micah 5:2
[146] Psalm 24:3-4
[147] 1 John 5:21
[148] 2 Timothy 2:22-26
[149] Psalm 12:6-7
[150] Psalm 24:3-6
[151] Genesis 4:4
[152] Genesis 4:7
[153] Isaiah 29:13, Matthew 15:8, Mark 7:6, Romans 6:17
[154] Acts 5:1-11
[155] Jonah 1:1-3, Matthew 12:41, Luke 11:32
[156] 2 Kings 5:1-17
[157] 2 Kings 5:13

158 Luke 4:7
159 Matthew 28:18-20
160 Genesis 12:1-3, 15:4-6, 17:1-16, 21:1-7, 21:12
161 Genesis 22:3
162 Genesis 22:5
163 Hebrews 11:17-19
164 Genesis 229-14
165 James 2:20-24
166 Genesis 22:18
167 Galatians 4:4-5
168 John 1:1-18
169 Hebrews 10:1-18
170 Matthew 3:13-17, 17:1-7, Mark 1:9-11, 9:2-13
171 John 8:58
172 John 6:38
173 Matthew 4:17
174 Matthew 26:36-46, Mark 14:32-42, John 18:1, Luke 22:39-41
175 Matthew 28:18b-20
176 John 12:49, 14:31
177 John 5:30, Revelation 21:18-19
178 Hebrews 5:9
179 Hebrews 12:11
180 Matthew 10:8
181 Isaiah 51:7
182 Ephesians 6:4, Proverbs 22:6
183 Titus 2:4
184 Proverbs 13:24
185 Ephesians 5:25-28
186 Ephesians 6:9
187 James 5:14, Hebrews 13:17, Titus 5-9, 1 Timothy 3:1-7, Ephesians 4:11
188 Hebrews 13:7-17
189 Hebrew 3:17-18, Titus 3:1-8
190 Ephesians 6:5-8
191 Titus 2:4-6
192 Colossians 3:20, Matthew 25:40
193 Hebrews 11
194 James 1:2-7
195 1 Peter 4:12-19
196 Matthew 28:20
197 Revelation 3:10
198 1 Corinthians 10:13
199 Hebrews 4:15, 7:25, Matthew 28:20
200 James 1:12-14
201 1 Corinthians 10:13
202 2 Peter 2-11

203 Deuteronomy 5:17
204 Genesis 9:5-7
205 Genesis 9:6, Revelation 21:8
206 Ephesians 5:6-14, Ezekiel 16:20-21
207 Exodus 21:22-25
208 1 Timothy 1:15
209 Stephen Boyd: "It's my body" is the devil's inversion of Christ's meaning when he spoke those words at Last Supper. Peter Kreeft: "Abortion is the Antichrist's demonic parody of the eucharist. That's why it uses the same holy words, 'This is my body,' with the blasphemous opposite meaning."
210 Psalm 127:3
211 Isaiah 44:24
212 Psalms 100:3
213 Job 31:15
214 Exodus 20:13
215 James 4:15-16 (NASB)
216 Philippians 2:3
217 1 Corinthians 6:20
218 1 Corinthians 6:9
219 Isaiah 44:1-2
220 Jeremiah 1:5
221 1 Corinthians 7:2-5
222 Psalm 119:97-105
223 Genesis 2:18
224 Genesis 2:18-20
225 Genesis 2:21-25
226 Genesis 2:15-17
227 Genesis 2:24, 4:1-2, 17:19, Exodus 20:12, Leviticus 19:3, Proverbs 6:20
228 Matthew 19:1-9
229 Titus 2:1-5
230 Genesis 2:1-17
231 John 1:1-5
232 1 Peter 1:20
233 Genesis 2:18-25
234 Ephesians 5:25, Revelation 21:2, 21:9, 22:17
235 Matthew 19:3-10
236 Exodus 20:5, 34:14, Deuteronomy 4:24
237 Proverbs 15:1
238 Galatians 5:19-26, Ephesians 5:1-16, John 8:44, 1 Peter 5:8
239 1 Corinthians 13:1-3
240 John 13:34

[241] Romans 13:10, 14:15, Ephesians 4:15, Colossians 3:12-17, Hebrews 6:10, 1 John 2:10, 3:10, 4:20-21
[242] 1 John 4:8, 4:16
[243] 1 Corinthians 13
[244] 1 Corinthians 13:4-5
[245] Ruth 4:18-22, Matthew 1:1-18, Luke 3:31-34
[246] 1 Corinthians 13:4, Colossians 3:5
[247] 1 Corinthians 13:4-7
[248] Ruth 1:16-17
[249] 1 Corinthians 13:5b-6a
[250] Though King David married several wives, Christ made it clear that, like divorce, polygamy was not God's plan.
[251] 1 Chronicles 15:29
[252] 2 Samuel 6:16-23
[253] 1 Samuel 25:2-43
[254] 1 Corinthians 13:6-8a
[255] Acts 18:3 Paul was a lawyer, but his formal education also included a manual trade. Paul supported himself with this work so he could preach without asking for support from those he was teaching.
[256] Acts 18:24-28
[257] Acts 18:18
[258] Romans 16:4
[259] 1 Corinthians 7:5
[260] Ephesians 5:22, Colossians 3:18
[261] 1 Peter 3:1-7
[262] Luke 2:49, John 5:30, 8:28, 10:18, 10:30-32, 12:49, 14:12, 14:24, 15:9, Matthew 26:39-42
[263] 1 Peter 5:5
[264] Titus 2:5
[265] Job 2:9
[266] Job 2:10
[267] Proverbs 18:22
[268] Proverbs 31:10-12, 31:30
[269] Proverbs 19:13
[270] 1 Timothy 5:8
[271] Philippians 2:3
[272] 1 Peter 3:7
[273] Ephesians 5:22–33
[274] Exodus 34:14, James 4:4
[275] Genesis 2:24–25
[276] Song of Solomon 4:11
[277] https://rlsglobalconsultinggov.com/faq/how-much-tax-money-goes-to-planned-parenthood-question.html, https://lozierinstitute.org/a-policy-and-funding-evaluation-of-human-fetal-tissue-research/, https://www.spectrumnews.org/news/trumps-fetal-tissue-policy-impacts-medical-research/
[278] U. S. Census Bureau (36% of marriages end in divorce, < 33% reach 25th anniversary)
[279] Romans 12:2
[280] 1 Timothy 5:9-10
[281] 1 Peter 3:12, 1 Corinthians 7:10-16
[282] 1 Corinthians 8:21
[283] Genesis 1:27, 5:2
[284] Mark 10:6, Matthew 19:8
[285] Matthew 19:7-9, Malachi 2:16, Mark 16:17-29, John 4:16-18
[286] Matthew 15:19, 1 Corinthians 6:9, 13-18, Galatians 5:19-21, Ephesians 5:5, Hebrews 13:4
[287] Ephesians 5:25-33, Colossians 3:19, Genesis 2:23-24
[288] John 3:16
[289] Titus 2:4
[290] Mark 12:30-33, Luke 10:27, Deuteronomy 6:55
[291] Matthew 25:34-46
[292] Luke 6:35
[293] Genesis 4:1, Deuteronomy 28:4, Psalms 127:3-5, Luke 1
[294] 1 Timothy 5:8
[295] Deuteronomy 4:9, 5:16, 6:1-9, 11:19, Joel 1:3, 2 Timothy 1:1-20, 3:16, Acts 17:10-11
[296] 1 John 3:10-11, 1 Corinthians 15:33, Psalm 1:1
[297] Ephesians 6:1-7, Hebrews 12:5-11, Proverbs 1:8-9, Hebrews 12:11
[298] Proverbs 22:6, Colossians 3:20-21, 1 Samuel 3:13, Proverbs 29:15-17, Proverbs 13:24
[299] Galatians 6:5, Ezekiel 18:20
[300] Genesis 2:24, Titus 2:4, Ephesians 5:33, 1 Corinthians 11:3, 1 Peter 3:1-7, Colossians 3:8

[301] Exodus 10:2, Proverbs 20:20, 30:17, Ezekiel 18:20, Matthew 15:4, Luke 12:48
[302] Genesis 19:19, Psalm 103:13, Matthew 6:34, 1 Timothy 5:10, 2 Timothy 1:5, 3:15, James 1:27
[303] Proverbs 23:22, John 19:25-27, Luke 2:51, 1 Timothy 5:4,
[304] Exodus 20:12, Isaiah 38:19, 3 John 1:4, 1 Corinthians 13:11
[305] Ephesians 6:4, Proverbs 19:26, 23:13-14, James 4:6, Luke 15:11-32, Acts 5:29, 1 Timothy 1:1-20, 2 Timothy 3:2, Romans 1:22
[306] Matthew 18:6-14, 25:24-29, Mark 9:42-48
[307] Isaiah 3:5, Proverbs 23:12-35
[308] Psalm 38:8-11
[309] Proverbs 22:6, 15
[310] Luke 18:15-17
[311] 1 Samuel 2:26
[312] Luke 2:52
[313] I Corinthians 13:11
[314] Mark 1:11
[315] Luke 15:17–19
[316] Luke 15:15:32
[317] Ephesians 6:11
[318] Psalm 119:142
[319] Mark 4:21-25
[320] 1 John 5:2-3, Deuteronomy 8:6, Ecclesiastes 12:13
[321] Psalm 1:2, Romans 7:22
[322] 1 Peter 5:8
[323] Mark 9:42, Romans 14:13
[324] Matthew 18:15-17, Galatians 6:1
[325] Matthew 7:3-4
[326] 1 Timothy 5:8, Mark 7:9-16
[327] Titus 2:6-7
[328] Hebrews 10:23-31, Ezekiel 18:20
[329] Deuteronomy 4:6-9
[330] 3 John 4
[331] Psalm 127
[332] Psalm 78:1-7
[333] Psalms 34:11–14
[334] Luke 2:36-38
[335] 1 Timothy 5:9-10
[336] Acts 2:44–47
[337] Luke 14:12–14
[338] Matthew 25:31-46
[339] Luke 11:9-13
[340] Acts 9:36-42
[341] John 6:9-14
[342] 1 Timothy 5:8-10
[343] Matthew 11:23-24, Luke 10:15
[344] Philemon 12-14
[345] Luke 21:1-4, Mark 12:41-45
[346] Ephesians 4:28
[347] 1 John 3:16-18vf
[348] Acts 4
[349] 2 Corinthians 9:5-15
[350] Psalm 112:9
[351] Matthew 25:40
[352] 1 John 4:7-11
[353] 1 Peter 4:7-10
[354] Psalm 112:1–10
[355] Matthew 16:18, Romans 6:9
[356] John 3:5, Matthew 6:33, 25:1 & 14, 26:29, Mark 1:15, Luke 1:33, 9:60, 16:16, 17:20-21, 2 Peter 1:10, Revelation 11:15
[357] John 15:12
[358] 1 John 3:3
[359] 1 John 2:1-6
[360] Matthew 13:3-9, 16:24, Luke 9:57-62, John 10:4-5
[361] Mark 8:35, Romans 6
[362] 1 Timothy 6:6-16
[363] Matthew 28:18
[364] John 6:57
[365] John 14:6
[366] John 14:3, 6
[367] Luke 9:23
[368] John 6:38
[369] John 5:30
[370] Matthew 7:21, Romans 12:2
[371] Luke 12:32-34
[372] Ephesians 5:22-28
[373] Colossians 3:22, Ephesians 6:5-6
[374] Matthew 19:29
[375] Luke 5:1-11
[376] Luke 5:8
[377] Matthew 4:19, Mark 1:17
[378] 1 Corinthians 3:6-7, 2 Corinthians 9:10
[379] John 5:36
[380] Matthew 4:17, 12:41, Mark 6:7-12, Luke 11:13, 24:46-48
[381] Matthew 22:35-40

BE KEEPERS

[382] Matthew 22:37-40, Deuteronomy 6:5
[383] Luke 13:31
[384] John 8:36, 15:15
[385] Mark 6:1-6
[386] Matthew 4:23, 9:35
[387] Matthew 8:3, Luke 7:1-10, 19:2-8, John 4—7, 8:1-11, Mark 7:24-30
[388] John 8:32
[389] Matthew 14:23, Luke 3:21, 4:18, 6:12, 9:18, 9:28, 11:1-4, 22:32, 22:40-46
[390] Philippians 2:8
[391] John 21
[392] Luke 14:11 and 18:14
[393] John 15:14
[394] 1 John 3:17, 4:20
[395] 1 John 1:7
[396] John 12:35
[397] Eph 2:10
[398] 2 Peter 2:20-22
[399] 1 John 3:10b
[400] 1 John 1:7
[401] 1 John 1:9
[402] Hebrews 6:4-6
[403] John 13:34, 1 John 2:8, 2 John 5, Galatians 2:20, Ephesians 4:11, 5:25, Titus 2:14
[404] James 2:4
[405] 1 Peter 2:9
[406] Genesis 4, 1 John 3:12, Mark 15:10, John 13:16, 15:20
[407] 1 Peter 3:18-22
[408] Matthew 8:22
[409] 1 Corinthians 10:21, Ephesians 5:7, 2 John 9-11
[410] Matthew 5:30, 18:8, 9:43-45
[411] Matthew 19:21, Mark 10:21
[412] Luke 18:28-30
[413] Mark 8:34
[414] Luke 17:33
[415] 1 Corinthians 13:1-13
[416] 1 Corinthians 13:4-7
[417] 1 Timothy 2:1-72 Timothy 2:15
[418] 1 Peter 2:2
[419] 1 Thessalonians 2:13
[420] Luke 12:34
[421] John 6:68, Philippians 2:16, 1 Peter 1:22-25
[422] Romans 1:16-17
[423] 1 Peter 1:23
[424] 1 John 2:5, 2:14
[425] 2 Peter 1:16
[426] Romans 12:2, 1 Corinthians 1:12, 2 Timothy 3:16
[427] 2 Timothy 3:5-6
[428] Romans 6:1-4
[429] 3 John 11
[430] Numbers 23:19
[431] Galatians 1:6-10
[432] Galatians 1:8-9, 2 Peter 2, Acts 11:17, Philippians 2:12
[433] 1 Thessalonians 1:6
[434] 1 Corinthians 11:1-3
[435] Hebrews 13:7, 2 Thessalonians 3:7-9
[436] 1 Corinthians 1:21, Romans 10:15
[437] James 3:1
[438] Luke 17:2, Romans 14:15, 1 Corinthians 8:11
[439] Philippians 2:5-11
[440] Genesis 3:20, Genesis 4:16-18
[441] Genesis 4
[442] Genesis 4:6-7
[443] Leviticus 10:1-5
[444] Leviticus 10:1-3
[445] John 7:26
[446] Ephesians 4:1-5, Colossians 3:15
[447] Acts 2:46-47.
[448] Matthew 1:36-43
[449] Malachi 3:18, Philippians 1:9-11
[450] Luke 6:21-23, Matthew 25:31-46
[451] Ephesians 6:10-13
[452] 2 Corinthians 10:1-6
[453] Colossians 2:11-15
[454] 2 Peter 3:14
[455] Luke 6:35
[456] Ezekiel 14:12-14
[457] John 13:34-35
[458] Hebrews 10:24-25
[459] 1 Corinthians 10:16-17
[460] James 5:16
[461] 1 Thessalonians 2:10-12
[462] Ephesians 4:11-12
[463] Colossians 3:16.
[464] 1 Corinthians 16:2
[465] Philippians 1:27-28

[466] 1 Thessalonians 5:11
[467] Romans 14:19
[468] 1 Peter 1:22
[469] Hebrews 11—12:3
[470] Colossians 3:12-16
[471] Mark 1:9-11
[472] 2 Corinthians 12:10
[473] John 13:34
[474] Genesis 4:9
[475] Matthew 12:37
[476] James 5:19-20
[477] Romans 14:21
[478] Romans 14:1-23
[479] John 13:35
[480] Exodus 17:8-16
[481] Ecclesiastes 4:11, Mark 6:7, Philippians 1:27
[482] 1 Thessalonians 5:12
[483] Romans 15:14
[484] Ephesians 4:11-16
[485] 2 Thessalonians 3:15
[486] 1 Corinthians 10:13
[487] Galatians 4:16
[488] James 5:20
[489] Matthew 7:5
[490] Acts 4:36-37
[491] Romans 16:3-4
[492] 1 John 3:16-17
[493] Jude 3
[494] 1 Timothy 2:1-4
[495] Hebrews 10:24-25
[496] Psalms 1:1-3
[498] Psalms 119:4, 1 Timothy 5:10, Hebrews 11:6
[499] Mark 16:15-16
[500] Matthew 28:18-20
[501] Mark 16:19-20
[502] 1 Corinthians 1:21
[504] 1 Timothy 2:11-12, 1 Corinthians 14:34-37
[505] Deuteronomy 4:9, 6:7
[506] Titus 2:1-5
[507] 1 Timothy 3:11
[508] 1 Timothy 1:5
[509] Acts 16:14-15, 40, Matthew 27:55, Mark 15:41, Philippians 4:3
[510] Hebrews 10:25
[511] John 4:28-30
[512] Acts 12:12-17, 1 Thessalonians 5:17
[513] Acts 9:36-39
[514] James 2:14-20, Romans 16:3, 1 Corinthians 3:9, 2 Corinthians 1:24, Philippians 4:3
[516] John 5:17
[517] Psalm 121:3-4
[518] Luke 12:6-7
[519] 1 Thessalonians 5:16-18
[520] Isaiah 59:1
[521] Genesis 18:14, Jeremiah 32:27, Luke 1:37, Hebrews 13:5
[522] Matthew 28:20
[523] John 6:29
[524] Matthew 21:28—23:3
[525] Luke 15:8-10
[526] Luke 15:1-7
[527] Luke 15:11-32
[528] 2 Thessalonians 3:10
[529] John 14:3-8
[530] 1 Timothy 5:13-14
[531] 1 Timothy 5:10
[532] 2 Corinthians 9:8
[533] John 3:16, 6:28-29, Acts 8:37, Romans 19:9-10, 1 John 5:13
[534] James 2:18-24
[535] Matthew 13:3-23, Mark 4:3-20, Luke 8:5-15
[536] James 1:17
[537] Romans 1:11
[538] Mark 6:7
[539] Luke 6:5, Matthew 6:20
[540] 1 Peter 5:6
[541] Mark 12:41-44, 14:4-9
[542] Mark 14:9, Matthew 26:13
[543] Mark 7:10, Exodus 20:12, 1 Timothy 5:3-4
[544] James 1:27
[545] Hebrews 6:10-20, Hebrews 6—10
[546] Matthew 13:43
[547] James 1:22-25
[548] James 2:14-17
[549] Psalm 18:28-29
[550] Romans 1:16-17
[551] John 14:6
[552] Acts 19:20, 19:23
[553] Hebrews 10:19-22
[554] Acts 20:7

555 Acts 11:26
556 1 John 3:1-3
557 1 Corinthians 1:2
558 1 Peter 2:11-12
559 Ephesians 5:25-27
560 1 Corinthians 1:4-9
561 2 Thessalonians 1:10-12
562 Ephesians 6:12
563 Revelation 4:8-11
564 Revelation 4:8
565 2 Samuel 22:4
566 Revelation 4:11
567 Revelation 5:9
568 Revelation 5:12
569 Revelation 5:13
570 Revelation 3:5
571 Matthew 22:8
572 Matthew 22:11-14
573 Galatians 3:26-27
574 Ephesians 2:4-10
575 Galatians 1:3-5
576 John 1:26-27
577 John 1:29-36
578 John 3:30
579 Isaiah 40:3
580 Malachi 4:5-6
581 Luke 1:39-45, John 1:28-35
582 Matthew 3:14
583 Luke 7:1-9
584 Isaiah 64:8
585 Isaiah 29:16
586 Isaiah 45:9
587 Isaiah 64:8
588 Luke 15:21
589 1 Thessalonians 2:10-12
590 Ephesians 4:1-6
591 Romans 16:2, Philippians 1:27, Colossians 1:10, 1 Thessalonians 2:12
592 Ephesians 5:15-17
593 Coffman, J. B. (1984). *Commentary on Galatians, Ephesians, Philippians, and Colossians*. A. C. U. Press.
594 Colossians 4:5-6
595 Ephesians 5:15-24
596 Romans 8:18
597 Romans 8:35-39
598 Titus 2:11-14
599 Ephesians 1:7
600 1 Peter 2:24
601 Genesis 2:16-17
602 Romans 6:23
603 Romans 3:23
604 John 14:6
605 Acts 4:12
606 1 John 5:12
607 Galatians 3:26-27
608 Ephesians 2:4-10
609 Psalms 18:1-3
610 Matthew 8:26
611 Matthew 10:29-31
612 Matthew 10:28-32
613 James 4:7
614 Matthew 16:18
615 Matthew 24:35, Mark 13:31, Luke 21:33
616 Revelation 2:10
617 Judges 14:5-14
618 2 Corinthians 12:10
619 Hebrews 11:7
620 Matthew 28:18-20, Mark 16:14-16
621 Romans 6:4-6, Colossians 2:12
622 1 John 1:7, Revelation 1:5
623 Romans 6:4
624 1 Kings 13:9
625 1 Kings 13:21-22
626 Galatians 1:8
627 Colossians 2:4, Hebrews 9:11-28
628 Hebrews 9:13-15
629 1 Corinthians 15:3-8
630 Acts 2:38-39.
631 Acts 10—11, 16:25-34
632 Acts 16:5, 18:8, 19:1-7, Romans 6:1-4, 1 Corinthians 12:13, Galatians 3:27
633 Romans 8:11, 1 Peter 3:18
634 1 Peter 3:20-22
635 Matthew 28:18-20
636 Hebrews 10:19-22: (alludes to Exodus 28:41, 29:21, 30:17-21)
637 2 Timothy 2:15
638 2 Thessalonians 2:3-11
639 Galatians 1:8-9
640 Colossians 2:8
641 Hebrews 6:1-3
642 Ephesians 4:3-7
643 Colossians 2:12

644 1 Corinthians 12:13
645 Matthew 28:20-21, Mark 16:15-16, Revelation 1:5
646 Philippians 2:12
647 Hebrews 2:1-4
648 1 John 4:17-19
649 Romans 8:15
650 Hebrews 12:1-11
651 Hebrews 12:11
652 Proverbs 13:24
653 Proverbs 15:10
654 Acts 3:19
655 Mark 15:43, Matthew 27:57-60
656 John 19:39
657 Psalm 27:1, Hebrews 13:6
658 2 Timothy 1:7-14
659 Acts 9:16, 2 Corinthians 11:22-33
660 Hebrews 12:22-24, 28—29
661 Psalms 27:1-14
662 Psalm 145:15-16
663 Revelation 22:20
664 Mark 13:32-37
665 Nehemiah 4:6
666 Nehemiah 6:16
667 Nehemiah 7:3
667 Nehemiah 8:1-3
668 Nehemiah 8:6
669 Nehemiah 8:9
670 Nehemiah 8:9-10
671 Acts 20:31
672 Luke 2:8-11
673 Matthew 26:40-41
674 Matthew 26:30-35, Luke 22:31-34
675 Matthew 24:45-51
676 Luke 12:35-38
677 Luke 12:40
678 Luke 21:34-36 (Matthew 24:36-44, Mark 13:31-37)
679 https://library.timelesstruths.org/music/Will_Jesus_Find_Us_Watching/score/
680 Luke 21:21
681 1 Corinthians 16:13-14
682 1 Thessalonians 5:6
683 Ephesians 6:14-20
684 2 Timothy 4:1-5
685 3 John 1:4
686 Hebrews 13:17
687 John 14:2-3
688 Daniel 12:1-3
689 Matthew 24:42
690 Mark 13:33
691 Mark 13:37
692 Hebrews 10:26-29
693 1 Peter 4:7-10
694 Harris, W. H., III, Ritzema, E., Brannan, R., Mangum, D., Dunham, J., Reimer, J. A., & Wierenga, M., eds. (2012). *The Lexham English Bible* (James 5:7-8). Lexham Press.
695 Jude 20-21
696 Revelation 3:3
697 1 Corinthians 13:12
698 Romans 8:38-39
699 Galatians 3:28
700 Matthew 5:4, 1 Peter 3:9, Romans 12:14
701 Romans 12:18
702 Ephesians 4:15, 1 Peter 3:15
703 1 Thessalonians 5:17
704 Titus 1:2 as variously translated: (NKJV), "in hope of eternal life which God, who cannot lie, promised before time began"; (ESV) "in hope of eternal life, which God, who never lies, promised before the ages began"; (YLT) "upon hope of life age-during, which God, who doth not lie, did promise before times of ages."
705 Matthew 6:33
706 Luke 11:9-10
707 Matthew 28:18-20
708 Mark 16:16
709 1 John 4:9
710 John 11: 25-26
711 Matthew 25:34
712 Numbers 23:19
713 Lamentations 3:22-24
714 2 Thessalonians 3:3
715 Hebrews 10:23
716 1 Corinthians 1:9
717 1 John 1:9
718 Psalm 119:89-90a
719 Genesis 37—50
720 Genesis 45:5-8
721 Genesis 50:19-21

BE KEEPERS

[722] Genesis 8:22, Nehemiah 9:21, Psalm 22:28, Matthew 6:19-33, Romans 8:28, 11:36
[723] Acts 7:9, Hebrews 7:4
[724] Acts 7:57–58
[725] 1 John 4:11, Matthew 5:44
[726] Romans 12:18
[727] Ephesians 4:15
[728] Matthew 7:7-11
[729] 1 Thessalonians 5:16-18
[730] Matthew 10:22
[731] Philippians 3:7-11
[732] Hebrews 13:5-6
[733] Deuteronomy 31:6
[734] 2 Timothy 1:7-12
[735] Revelation 2:10
[736] Revelation 3:10
[737] John 18:36
[738] John 17:9-20
[739] 2 Peter 3:13
[740] Hebrews 13:14
[741] John 14:1–3
[742] Titus 3:4-7
[743] Revelation 3:5
[744] 1 Corinthians 2:9
[745] Hebrews 3:6
[746] Psalms 145:1–21
[747] Hebrews 4:12

www.ingramcontent.com/pod-product-compliance
Lightning Source LLC
Chambersburg PA
CBHW070611170426
43200CB00012B/2650